PRAISE FOR CHRIS DOMBROWSKI'S
Body of Water

"Dombrowski's writing exhibits a poetic sense of economy. There's a tremendous amount of information here on the geological, botanical, biological and human history of the region, but the author uses only what's necessary to the story and relates it in evocative, concise language that reminded me of Gary Snyder one minute and John McPhee the next. . . . Dombrowski's exacting descriptions of the sport make me long to try it again—and to wish that more fishing books were written by poets."

—JOHN GIERACH, *WALL STREET JOURNAL*

"*Body of Water* is wonderful, an evocation of the *why* and not the *how* in angling. Dombrowski has a way of describing that which may have become prosaic for the seasoned angler—the terminal tackle, the fly cast—in new and illuminating ways."   —*FORBES*

"This gorgeous work wastes not a word on fly-fishing basics. It dives *Moby-Dick* deep into a famed sport and livelihood's very essence, and never leaves. Via the hearts of two men utterly in love with the wounded world in which their calling takes place, *Body of Water* pours forth beauties, subtleties, dark history, and insight with an unforced lyrical power I associate with no lesser word than 'masterpiece.' Dombrowski's Michigan-to-Montana trajectory updates Jim Harrison, his comedic fishing scenes bear comparison to Thomas McGuane, and his powers of ebullient reflection bring to mind Mary Oliver—yet I've read no book anything like *Body of Water*, and enjoyed no book in memory more."

—DAVID JAMES DUNCAN, AUTHOR OF *THE RIVER WHY*

"This is some of the best writing that you'll ever read about fishing. But *Body of Water* achieves even more—it's a passionate, luminous, completely delightful book."

—IAN FRAZIER, AUTHOR OF *TRAVELS IN SIBERIA*

"*Body of Water* is about bonefishing, but it is also about ecosystem exploitation, class conflict, wealth inequity, race relations, Bahamian history, mentor-mentee relationships, nature as the catalyst for self-awareness, and more. . . . The lyrical narrative strikes a delicate balance between reflective memoir and reportage."

—*MINNEAPOLIS STAR TRIBUNE*

"Dombrowski elevates the fly-fishing-as-meditation narrative by the sheer fact that he's so damn good at writing about it. There's prose and practicality in equal parts, so the allure of the sport comes through." —*OUTSIDE*

"A metaphor-laced meditation on the art and practice of fly-fishing, the social and economic history of the Bahamas, the evolution of archipelago geology and the chronicle of Dombrowski's personal struggle to juggle his fishing and poetry obsessions against the financial needs of his own family . . . Fly-fishing mysticism at its best." —*SHELF AWARENESS*

"Dombrowski has fetched up a marvel. So very much is in it—geology, biology, fishing lore; conservation and natural history and personal quest—all seen by a wondrously limber mind traversing space and time. I don't fish but this scarcely matters—*Body of Water* is about being alive. An abundant and reverential feast of a book." —NOY HOLLAND, AUTHOR OF *BIRD*

"Rarely do cautionary tales dazzle like this. It's a credit to Dombrowski's prose, which torques and twists and glistens into view much like the bonefish itself. . . . By book's end, Dombrowksi leaves readers with many lessons, though this one most of all: whether on a skiff or in a book, the guide matters. And Dombrowski's the one you want." —*LOS ANGELES REVIEW*

"Dombrowski adeptly shifts focus between a microscopic fascination with the natural world and the vast frames of racial oppression, conservation, and ecotourism. . . . He leaves many lines in the water for readers as well as fish: David Pinder's story of success and struggle within a racially divided industry, his own identity as both writer and guide, and the story of the bonefish in its ancient watery world. We follow each of these captivating hooks from depths to surface." —*HIGH DESERT JOURNAL*

"At its core, *Body of Water* is about our increasingly tenuous connection to nature, from a poet who understands the source of that strange and melancholic joy that we are blessed with only when we stand in wild places." —STEVEN RINELLA, AUTHOR OF *MEAT EATER*

"Uncanny and moving. This book will not only make you change your vacation plans, it might make you change your life. A reverent, almost holy book, of angling lore." —DEBRA MAGPIE EARLING, AUTHOR OF *PERMA RED*

"A lyrical, genre-defying tribute . . . Drawing on Caribbean history and the evolution of fly-fishing, Dombrowski's foray into nonfiction proves thematically complex, finely wrought, and profoundly life-affirming." —*PUBLISHERS WEEKLY* (STARRED REVIEW)

BODY *of* WATER

BODY *of* WATER

A Sage, a Seeker, and the World's Most Alluring Fish

CHRIS DOMBROWSKI

MILKWEED EDITIONS

First paperback edition, published 2017 by Milkweed Editions
Printed in the United States of America
Cover and interior design by Mary Austin Speaker
Typeset in Adobe Jenson Pro
Cover photo by Andy Anderson
Author photo by Erik Peterson
17 18 19 20 21   5 4 3 2 1

978-1-57131-364-5

Milkweed Editions, an independent nonprofit publisher, gratefully acknowledges sustaining support from the Jerome Foundation; the Lindquist & Vennum Foundation; the McKnight Foundation; the National Endowment for the Arts; the Target Foundation; and other generous contributions from foundations, corporations, and individuals. Also, this activity is made possible by the voters of Minnesota through a Minnesota State Arts Board Operating Support grant, thanks to a legislative appropriation from the arts and cultural heritage fund, and a grant from the Wells Fargo Foundation. For a full listing of Milkweed Editions supporters, please visit milkweed.org.

Library of Congress Cataloging-in-Publication Data

Names: Dombrowski, Chris, 1976- , author.
Title: Body of water / Chris Dombrowski.
Description: First edition. | Minneapolis, Minnesota : Milkweed Editions, 2016.
Identifiers: LCCN 2016015127 (print) | LCCN 2016031357 (ebook) | ISBN 9781571313522 (cloth) | ISBN 9781571319159 (e-book)
Subjects: LCSH: Bonefishing—Bahamas—Grand Bahama—Anecdotes. | Fishing guides—Bahamas—Grand Bahama—Anecdotes. | Pinder, David. | Dombrowski, Chris, 1976- | Bonefish.
Classification: LCC SH691.B6 D66 2016 (print) | LCC SH691.B6 (ebook) | DDC 639.2/7097296—dc23
LC record available at https://lccn.loc.gov/2016015127

For the Pinder family
and for my father, who took me fishing,
even in the rain

Contents

Far Country

From ancient times wise people and sages have often lived near water. When they live near water they catch fish, catch human beings, and catch the way.

DOGEN, "MOUNTAINS AND WATERS SUTRA"

BODY *of* WATER

Prologue

The man steps barefoot through shallow water, moving as if he carried a candle threatening to expire. He lifts his left foot from the ankle-deep slack tide and holds it poised in the early-morning air until the last drops from his pant cuff return to the salt. Then he advances, setting his foot down toes first, dark brown on the pale Caribbean sand.

Now he stands so still a passing cormorant might light and perch on his shoulder, mistaking man for mangrove.

Now he proceeds.

So that a single bonefish feeding along the tidal flat's periphery won't startle, he walks this way; so his wake won't alert the nearby assemblage of mojarras, the myriad minnow eyes trained already on his shadow. He holds the borrowed fly rod behind his back, a strange nine-foot tail, so that its lacquered finish won't redirect sunlight toward the fish. Again he steps, closing the distance between his body and his quarry's hovering form, its bottom-cast penumbra.

Sensing danger, the fish maintains shrewd space and near invisibility. Since it arrived on the flat, the five dark vertical stripes have disappeared from its flanks, and before that its scales maintained the hue of the narrow blue defile it negotiated on its way to these shallow feeding grounds. Now its sides are star white, chalky, its location perpetually vague and mirroring whatever surrounds it until it tilts, nose down, to root a bellicose crab from a burrow. Then its sloped back and dorsal fin cut through the surface, light shellacked, announcing its location to the airy world.

Its tail shimmers, a loose-fitting bracelet affixed to the wrist of a beautiful woman seated at a bar, the likes of whom the man has seen only in movies, or through the dining room window of the fishing club where he works. Before the foraging fish, a puff of inhaled sand the fish's gills expel, clouding its vision. The man gains a yard while the water clears and the fish finishes pulverizing the crab with the crunchers in the back of its throat. Then he stills again and waits until the hovering fish inverts its nose, now pink from the rooting, toward another meal.

Low on the horizon, a single crown-shaped cloud lifts toward the rising sun. The man's sighting light is limited; when the cumulus obscures the sun, the water's surface will turn opaque, gray as a blind eye. The tide is due to turn and the south wind, low now but sure to advance with the day, will harry the incoming water onto the flat, pushing the lone fish into an apse of mangroves, a maze of many-fingered roots. Small, eager snappers will emerge there, busying the water, quick to jump on his offering before his fish has a chance. Schools of loose-scaled green fry frequent the cove as well, behind which the big predatory Cubera are never far—once he saw a fifteen-pounder annihilate a whole school: when it finally settled, the water looked strewn with tiny emeralds.

"Get yourself another crab," he whispers, and commences tugging twenty reams of yellow fly line from the Medalist reel seated at the base of the rod. The reel's gears click slightly as he pulls—he looks to see if this has altered the fish's posture, but the fish seems unbothered. Soon the loose fly line lies in coils in the water around his ankles, and he holds the fly in his hand, letting ten feet of clear monofilament leader dangle like a luffing sail at his side.

Fortune: the fish has tipped down again to feed, this time with its tail facing toward him. He takes two careful steps and begins his back-cast, extending his right forearm out and upward from his elbow, flexing the fiberglass rod deeply so that, springing, it propels the slack line behind him. The line straightens, bristling with water like a long, lit wick.

Here the fully extended back-cast, waiting for the forward

cast to propel it to its destination, breathes: a pause, an emptiness at the root of which all good lies.

The forward cast: a tug against the tension the back-cast established, a punch through the humid air that cannons the poised line forward parallel to the water. Because the edgy fish navigates such a shallow element, the man knows his fly must land like a feather—it must alight, not land. He finishes his cast high, right hand reaching above his head so that the forward-traveling line extends upward and outward from his body, and the fly at the end of the tippet at the end of the leader at the end of the line lists toward the water before landing, a detectable but not irksome disturbance.

The fish turns, scurries a short yard to the south, and puts eyes on it: a stainless steel hook wrapped with brown thread, two upwardly pointing tips of hackle borrowed from a rooster's cape, and a set of brass bead-chain eyes wrapped liberally with pink chenille yarn. A shrimp in flight, a crab wielding its pincers, a benthic worm protruding from a hole in the seafloor: the man couldn't care less what forage the fish mistakes the fly for, so long as it's taken. Now his rod hand and line hand come together as if in the briefest of prayers, and he gives the loop of line below the reel a tug, so that the lure dashes across the sand in irresistible faux flight.

Dithering, the fish stares squarely at the fly, but before the man can play puppeteer again, it pivots its body to inhale. The man feels the pulse-like thump that tells him fish jaw has ceded to hook point, and, tugging again, feels the sweet stretch of the monofilament leader travel through rod blank and cork handle to hand. The fish torques, readies its body to burst for the horizon; the man raises his now equally torqued fly rod, and the line connecting two creatures—across which the sun's ancient and instant light stretches—comes taut.

BEGINNER'S

MIND

Tablet

If you find you no longer believe enlarge the temple.

—W. S. MERWIN

On still mornings like this one, from the McLean's Town dock you can watch a single fold of water rolling in from a long way off and wonder where, how far out there, it began its approach. Like any story, this wave begins at an arbitrary point: before it was a wave closing in on the shore, it was an exhalation, and before it was a breath it was a drop of rain, a skein of clouds, a pothole lake, a snowfield at elevation. For all intents and purposes, it always was, never wasn't. Look: already it's a modest swash breaking over the blanched sand on my bare feet, receding seaward.

I first came to the East End of Grand Bahama Island to fish, a little less than a decade ago. Escapee from a soul-sapping Rocky Mountain winter, I arrived that April on the trade wind of a friend's generosity—*So-and-so can't go, it's all paid for*—a gift that couldn't have arrived in a timelier fashion. I was about to enter my thirteenth year as a fly-fishing guide in Montana, but would have to wait two months before my seasonal work began in earnest, and wait twice that many months before I could begin to row my way out of five-figure-deep debt, the product of some of my patented financial wizardry, which was itself largely a product of having indentured myself to the angling life at age sixteen, followed by sustained attempts to live like a sixteen-year-old for the ensuing seventeen years.

To complicate fiscal matters, February had seeped into my bloodstream, the snow spindrifting off the wind-hardened backyard mounds like elemental enactments of my unstable

psychological state. And my young family needed not listless-
ness but some semblance of solidity from me: my wife Mary
and I had a young son and were expecting a second child, which
was worrisome not only because of my tenuous financial state,
but also because Mary's previous pregnancy had been fraught
with health complications. The thought of her spending several
months on bed rest again, on unpaid leave from her job—our
only steady income—deadened me with fear. I think it's fair to
say now, with the perspective several years afford, that I was at
best clinically depressed, fatigued with indecision that bordered
on dread, and in need of professional help.

My psychologist father could have referred me to any
number of well-qualified counselors. But out of some strange
instinct or allegiance, I trusted only water's treatments. Threadbare, more than a bit benumbed, I hoped I might be able to fish
myself out of my fret-driven depression. I'd done it before, each
cast a pathway out of what I assumed was myself. I remembered
vaguely, or perhaps had invented, an apocryphal story in which
doctors in ancient India tied mentally ill patients to trees beside
the moving water. Sequestered near the sound of water running
over rocks, the mad were often cured. I was hoping to fill such
a prescription.

"NO EXPECTATIONS," I PREACH TO CLIENTS ARRIVING TO
fish Montana's fabled rivers for the first time, but even on the
night flight from Miami to Grand Bahama, somewhere above
the black water between the hundred-mile torch of artificial
light that is the Florida coast and the relative candle that is Freeport, I found my own credo impossible to follow. Somewhere
below the plane swam actual schools of a silver fish that had
navigated the waters of my imagination for decades; I'd spent
entire winters reading books and lore about the bonefish, and

heard enough firsthand accounts of its caginess and speed that my mind's eye could effortlessly conjure images of that which I had neither hooked nor held, and that had not, to steal a phrase from Keats, been proved upon the pulses.

By the time the shuttle van neared McLean's Town the following morning I was twitchy as a dowser near a spring. In the front seat sat my host and longtime client Miller, an annual visitor to East End flats, who prepped me on the nuances of his home-away-from-home water much the way I had for him on our drives to the Bitterroot or Blackfoot. To further distract myself from impatience, I engaged our shuttle driver Freddi in a friendly debate over the NBA's best sixth man, and was arguing Dennis Rodman to his Kevin McHale as the van pulled into the docks.

"Shit!" Miller said with a start, slamming his hands on the van's dashboard. I figured he'd forgotten his wallet or passport, or worse yet his fishing rod, back at the hotel. "Excuse my language, Freddi," he said, "but I should stop at David Senior's and pay my regards. Just for a minute. Do you mind?"

"Of course not, Miller. I'll just put the old Odyssey in reverse. Tell me if I'm gonna hit a dog."

"Hey," Miller said, turning to lift his sunglasses and look me in the eyes, "you ought to come meet David. He's the guy that started all of this."

It was half past eight in the morning and I was desperate to set foot on my first Bahamian bonefish flat. I had traveled two thousand miles the previous day, crossed two time zones, cleared customs after midnight, and awoken at five a.m. in a hotel bed made frigid by extremely industrious air-conditioning fearing that I would miss my alarm and thus the shuttle—I knew the guide boats would be waiting for us across the channel, ready to leave the docks as soon as we dumped our luggage and donned some fishing pants. I excused my impatience with Miller's errand and remained in the van to organize my fly box.

Miller got out and walked through a yard strewn with bric-a-brac, car parts, and boat motor guts to the door of a bright-blue house. I watched in the rearview as he knocked and waited. A tall Bahamian man opened the door and squinted at the light, tucked in the tails of his plaid shirt, and extended his hand. He smiled—his close-cropped gray hair glowing like a newborn's—and with his free hand clasped Miller's shoulder, as Miller did the same to him. In the windshield view, a long fly cast from the van, a cormorant fell into flight from its mangrove perch. The bird thrashed the water's calm surface with its wingtips before angling up the bight. Sunlight pierced a distant wall of cumulus and fanned out across the water. Miller walked toward us in the rearview, and I saw the door of the blue house close.

AS OUR SKIFF CROSSED AN UNDERWATER TERRACE, I FELT a kind of spoiled guilt at my remove from whatever I had previously considered the world—the water beneath us resembled glacial ice, and the ocean floor's relief was an inverse of the elevation, the contours of my country. Our guide Meko Glinton—only thirty, but already a legend in the angling world and favored guide at the storied Deep Water Cay Club—cut the motor and let the boat coast shoreward toward a latticework of tiny channels running through the mangroves. Stalling the skiff finally with a long push-pole made of shaved pine, Meko asked me to slip off the bow and station myself ten yards downlight from the boat, on a small alcove of sand the skiff couldn't reach.

I had been briefed to think that Bahamian bonefish would be nearly impossible to see, but the tail of my first shone like a knife rinsed at a sunlit tap: a gimme from the fish gods for the rookie. In a mild chaos of shadow and waking water, more bones shot up the runnels into a tidal pool, their fleeting locations made known by Meko, who now stood well above the water, his thin frame hunched heron-like on his skiff's poling platform. He hollered and aimed the push-pole: four more fish had banked toward me.

I began to false-cast, casually measuring line to what seemed a proper distance, easing into the rhythm of the presentation, but Meko yelled, "This time!" jarring me from my trance. Released, my top-heavy cast seemed destined to spook the torsional fish. A headwind, though, sudden and warm, erected an invisible wall that the weighted fly banked off and slid down, so that the shallow water barely registered its entry. Shimmering, a bonefish levitated and inverted to take the fly, its tail severing the water's surface. I struck and the hook knocked in; after a wild fight, I beached the fish alongside some weathered coral rubble. The color of its scales recalled the face of a man deprived of oxygen.

While hooked, my fish had spooked its schoolmates and so we left the flat for another. Motoring through the maze of cays, we passed a small encampment of homes on Sweetings Cay, its church and bar; a dozen rusted buoys and one human-assembled cairn of conch shells; an engine prop's signature on the seafloor—but no further evidence of society's handprints on the landscape. As the boat halved a flock of banking curlews, Miller and I turned our heads to watch the flock reunite.

"Not much has changed in thirty-five years," he yelled into my ear over the engine noise. He waved his hand at the cay-dotted horizon. "Or two hundred for that matter."

He told me he had invited Meko and Meko's wife, Samantha, to dinner that night, across the channel from the lodge, to a place called Alma's. A diner, he allowed, but Alma's lobster was better than the club's. "The club gets a little miffed when we head across to eat, but it's tradition.

"I'm hoping David Senior will come, too," he said, adding that David was Meko's grandfather, and "the guy whose house we stopped at this morning. Literally the first bonefish guide in the Bahamas. The reason we're all here. I fished with him every year before he retired. Remind me, when were you born?"

I told him.

"Hell, I fished with David Senior before you were born. Over three decades ago, when my old man first brought me down. His eyesight's awful now. Cataracts. But he has wonderful stories. If he comes, you'll sit next to him. Guide meets guide."

THE SUN SANK, DIMINISHED, AND EVENING'S COOL FELL IN. Water-tired, the rock of the wave-cresting skiff in my bones, I sat at the dinner table, which overflowed with loud conversation and the promised lobster, as well as poached red snapper, its fins the color of my neck after initial exposure to Bahamian sun, the skin under my shirt collar radiating with warmth. We ate under an awning in plastic chairs around a picnic table covered in a plastic gingham tablecloth. Dressed in khakis and a white pearl-button snap shirt, David didn't say much but leaned in to listen to our talk, and each time he cleared his throat, or said so much as "Pass the salt and pepper, please," Meko and several other local guides at the table went reverently silent, their glory stories put on hold. After a while I felt obliged to include the elder statesman in the conversation, so I asked David to tell me one of the wildest things he'd witnessed in his four decades of guiding: a trivial question, but I couldn't think of another way to lure him out.

Fully functional or not, David's cataract-lidded eyes bored straight into mine, as if my pupils were something of great interest to him, as if they were a pair of tailing bonefish he did not want to lose sight of.

"One time, we were up north near Water Cay and a guest caught a very big bonefish, eleven pounds, if I remember. Fat fish. Looked like it was about to burst. Back then, club rules, guides could keep one fish. Usually we didn't clean it till we got to the dock, but its belly was squirming, this way and that. I had gaffed the fish and thought the wiggling was nerves, but the guest said no, he'd never seen nerves like that. So I gutted it. And you know what was in the belly of this eleven-pounder? One-pound bonefish. Still breathing! Yessir. I put the little guy back in the water, but he wasn't really swimming, just kind of floating there, working his gills.

"Who knows," David said, without a wink, with a guile-less grin that lifted the thin moustache he wore and revealed his front teeth, yellow as antique piano keys, and the vast gap between them. "Maybe he made it."

He passed a platter of conch.

"My daughter and I brought that up today. Ceviche," he said, his eyes flashing vibrantly for a brief instant—the flash the sun makes as it sets behind the sea.

I put a forkful in my mouth and chewed.

THAT NIGHT AFTER DINING WITH DAVID, ASLEEP IN A modest white cottage on Deep Water Cay, I dreamed I was walking atop the ridge of a dune. Gulls were everywhere, loud and swooping low. Someone else walked along the shoreline below me. My dream camera panned closer, and I could see a teenage girl, talking on a phone, smiling. The wind was blowing, especially through her hair. Even deep in the midst of sleep, I felt a prescient shiver of recognition: the young woman was the child Mary presently carried, somewhere in the future, alive, healthy.

I lurched up in bed as if commanded, and stepped across the cool terra-cotta tiles to the door. Outside I walked a hun-dred feet to the shore at the island's south side. Low on the barely lightening horizon a little *ceja* moon, new, was about to set, Venus winking to the east. Dawn was nearing, the humid air saturated with the wild din of peepers and crickets in their final act paired with birds announcing light's arrival.

I felt light, disburdened, and reasoned beyond logic that such a potent dream could have been bestowed on me only by this place, which now seemed vaguely familiar. I did what seemed appropriate: shucked my T-shirt and dunked—full immersion—three times, in the warm shallows. I looked out across the sheer flat for a sign of the fish I had journeyed so far to catch—from foot to horizon, the water looked like a tablet with utter nothingness carved into it.

I had eaten dinner with a man who I reckoned knew more about that tablet than I could ever guess. He had given me one tale. I wondered what more he might be inclined to share.

Holocene

The fashioner of things has no original intentions.

—WANG WEI

Always the tide: two low, two high each day. Rising tide climbs into flood, which flushes into high, when the moon above is at its zenith, or passing underfoot at its nadir; then falling tide recedes into ebb, which bellies out to low, before the heavy pause that is slack tide, before the moon begins to tug again, a distant rock stirring water that stirs sand that once was rock.

Back home in Montana I unfolded the map of Grand Bahama frequently, and imagined the water pushing inland, then falling back from the mass of land that looked a little like a swordfish with an upturned bill, minus a fin or two. Near the bottom tip of the fish's crescent tail sat East End, where David had resided for an epoch. Even my puerile three-course under-graduate geology background, though, reminded me that the limestone platform on which he walked had existed far longer than he, or even the bonefish, could fathom. I dug back into my old textbooks, stole off to the library and thumbed through the vacant stacks like a student with a prof's merciful offer to retake a flunked final exam—not to raise some long-forgotten grade, but to give some footing to the water's story, some ground to a compelling man's steps. Tell me the landscape in which he lives, in other words, and I will tell you who he is.

Of course terms like *Late Jurassic* and *Cretaceous* mean little to nongeologists, and numbers of years ago like sixty or eighty million mean much less to mortals such as myself who can't account for yesterday. Suffice to say this limestone underlay

composed of the skeletal remains of barnacles and other immo-
bile organisms—minuscule wildflowers pressed between the
pages of a tome—has existed for an incomprehensibly long
period, and today measures nearly five miles in thickness.

Eventually this slab became so dense that it began to
subside under its own weight at a rate of roughly four centimeters per thousand years. For eons, though, the seafloor
simply spread warm waters farther and farther inland. This
was back when all the world was hot and humid, awash in
salty water. Huge toothy creatures swam here, stomped the
boggy shorelines. They ate foliage and each other, gnashed
bloodied teeth. They moved loudly and terribly, or so we
imagine and conjecture. We know them by their coveted
bones and fossils, and though the record of their massive
comings and goings is faint, we hear echoes of it in the roar
of heavy breakers rolling shoreward.

Then, like something out of a story I might tell my children
by the fire—something sudden, meant to terrify—a large, audibly flaming object plummeted from the sky, rent the ground,
and put an end to these creatures and to most breathing for a
while: to the braiding flights of birds and the small mammals
birthing nursing babies, to most green and flowering things.

But the water remained water, just as the rock, though
scarred, remained rock. Over another unfathomable stretch of
time, under great tectonic force—a tremendous focalization of
subterranean energy—the earth's crust buckled like pond ice
ceding to warm rain. The seafloor shifted, configuring banks,
and when the seas finally receded, the highest ridges formed
islands atop endless limestone shallows, the *Gran Bajamar*, as
the Spanish sailors called them millennia later, "Great Shallows," and eventually the Grand Bahama Bank.

By and by rain fell on the exposed bedrock and dissolved its
bonds, the falling water absorbing traces of atmospheric carbon

dioxide as it descended. When rain met limestone, they brewed a strange tea of weak carbonic acid that chewed through parts of the rock. Gem-blue holes were carved in the karst, adorning the seafloor with deep pools divers would covet centuries later.

More importantly from a biological perspective, a relatively thin but essential freshwater lens formed when the rainwater that had seeped through the limestone's surface collected below sea level, floating atop the denser salt water. This seminal meniscus of groundwater would come to comprise the majority of naturally occurring potable water in the islands, a fertile layer of liquid in which marine organisms large and small flourish. Its existence allows a would-be moonscape to morph into one of the world's most fecund habitats, a place where plants like mangrove trees thrive.

Amphibious trees that root in the unfriendliest of shoreline soils where no other tree can, mangroves can live for a hundred years. Subject to the conditions a mangrove endures daily— muck, salt, tidal fluctuations—an ordinary plant would wilt within a week, but mangroves don't only survive, they transform and soften the elements around them. Serving as natural head-walls, their banks protect inland ecosystems from rough seas and filter the negative constituents from the water, increasing the quality and volume of the freshwater lens. Inevitably salt permeates the trees' root systems, but they simply store it in old leaves, which they shed. And the mangroves' roots breathe, literally snorkeling for air while simultaneously anchoring the trees in tide-shifted mud. Crabs and snails climb and fasten themselves to these roots to avoid predators; these filter-feeding organisms also clean the water that flows back and forth over them, so that the tide can rush out cleansed into a thriving sea.

In the hour-long film that is Earth's history, we humans make our cameo in the final second. Perhaps that's why a phrase like *a rate of roughly four centimeters per thousand years* falls on deaf ears. We may never possess the genius of the mangroves and their adaptive ingenuity, but we may still have time to recognize our minuscule role in the order of things. The close study of a landscape such as this union of bedrock, tree, tidal flux, and fertile water is a start, and might lead us to move with the measure of the waters and the islands themselves.

Albula vulpes

A fish together with other fish invariably knows what
is on each other's mind. Unlike humans they are not
ignorant of each other's intentions.

—DOGEN ·

I sat often at my computer looking at the picture turned screen
saver that Miller had sent of me holding my first bonefish,
my eyes beaming over soon-to-be-sunburned cheeks. Though
I'd caught thousands of fish in my lifetime, I'd doubted I'd ever
been so elated about one that so closely resembled a minnow.
Lacking the dangerous stiletto-shaped allure of a barracuda,
say, or the simple polished-penny sheen of a redfish, or the
azure panache of a dorado's dorsal fin, the bonefish possesses
the beauty, rather, of certain mirrors or windows.

Despite its homely appearance, its mouth shaped, in one
writer's words, "like a rechargeable vacuum cleaner," and its
relatively modest average size, the bonefish has attained sport
fish–royalty status due largely to its fickle manner and unsur-
passed acceleration. With sturdy caudal fins fanning winglike
from its flanks, the fish is built for departure. Tail tip to sloped
nose, its belly is nearly level, recalling, in profile, *Pterrichthyodes,*
"the first fish," which swam early seas 350 million years ago.

Weighing only a third of a pound in salt water, a fusiform
bonefish of six pounds shuns its element. Fleeing boat or boat's
shadow, a lemon shark or a conspiring pair of barracuda, the
bonefish can reach speeds of up to twenty-five miles per hour
swimming in water that is 760 times denser than air—I would
have to sprint at an equivalent speed through waist-deep Jell-O
to experience similar resistance.

When not fleeing danger, the bonefish avoids it by means of intricate disguise, its shadow nearly always more visible than its body. Over white sand, the fish appears the color of watered-down skim milk; over turtle grass, on a knee-deep subaqueous prairie, the fish jewels up, turning the color of some yet-to-be-discovered gem; traversing coral heads or mangrove roots, the fish goes sepia, the density of the pigment cells beneath its fingernail-shaped scales varying from moment to moment to match its environment.

Because of its considerable speed, the bonefish is rarely pursued in blue water by its predators. On the flats, however, the more herdable bone becomes a mark for teams of blacktip sharks, bonnetheads, and lemons. Ospreys traffic the air above shallow saltwater acreages, but rarely seek out adult bonefish when easier game abounds. The archipelago's first people netted bonefish, making the quarry keener to shore-walking humans' thudding vibrations—vibrations sensed in the fish's lateral line, a thin, tail-to-cheek organ that detects movements in the water. Centuries later the disturbing plop of a bell sinker followed shortly by the slightly quieter but equally alarming smack of a shrimp-threaded bait hook were added to this list of affronting sounds, the many suggestions of imminent death.

If desperate for safety, the fish seeks out like company: more eyes to watch for danger, more sensory organs alert. Despite its tendency to school, Linnaeus named the bonefish after a solitary mammal, and a conspicuous one at that: the white fox. The eighteenth-century naturalist, of course, had never seen an actual bonefish, and must have focused on sketches of the fish's canine nose. In Central America the bonefish is called *ratón* for the way it scurries briskly from the minutest piscatory failings. Among anglers, gray ghost is the preferred and perhaps most telling moniker; it is rarely visible to the average human eye, and a sighted fish is usually a fish in flight.

． ． ．

OUT IN THE BLUE WATER, FAR OFFSHORE AND FAR BENEATH the swelling surface of the sea, a large school of bonefish has gathered in the September dusk to spawn. A thousand or more staging fish, uniform in length as bars of silver. Through a paling shaft of light, the shimmering tornado made of scales and fins and eyes moves hypnotically, slowly circling an invisible axis. As the full moon lifts, the fish one by one abandon their rotation, rising toward the roof of their world to breach and gulp air, which helps males and females expel, respectively, sperm and roe that drop together from the cusp of an underwater terrace—hundreds of millions of eggs falling through spreading clouds of milt.

For several weeks the fertilized eggs rest on the ocean floor's good darkness, in one of the few places we know blessedly little about. Then from the eggs heads and ink-splotch eyes protrude as the fish begin their forty-day larval stage, expanding in this form until they are two inches long and metamorphosis begins. Before they continue to grow, they must shrink—maturing implausibly in reverse, contracting through the leptocephalid stage over a ten-day period. Nourished on plankton, they soon look quite like miniature, one-inch bonefish, creatures protected by the same number of scales from birth to death.

BONEFISH SURVIVING THREE DOZEN MOONS WITHIN THE relative protection of mangrove swamps will mature sexually and grow into one of the world's most coveted game fish—such as the flat-foraging specimen I cast toward now, which, curse instinct, disengages from its school and mistakes this traveling angler's artificial fly for a live, fleeing shrimp. When the false prey is attacked, a steel hook dressed with feathers bites into the fish's bony palate.

Quickened along with the fish, I brace against its first blistering run, wet line peeling off the reel and spraying onto my face and polarized lenses. Very soon the fish is farther out than I can see, struggling against the rod's full bend to reach the edge of the flat where the seafloor falls abruptly into the fathom-deep green. Like exaggeratedly slow seconds ticking off on a watch, line clicks off the reel one gear rotation at a time. As the distance increases, so does the tension on the line, on the knot joining monofilament leader to fly. For a hundred yards—from fish to fist gripping rod cork, from shoulder to heel seated in the sand—there is connection, like a long tendon, stressed to its tearing point.

This tug, as anglers visiting the islands say, "is the drug," a quick hit of adrenaline initiated by a hooked and fleeing bonefish, and one the Bahamian tourism industry counts as an invaluable commodity, having recently gauged the industry surrounding the scarcely edible fish at roughly $150 million annually.

I lean the rod low and the fish finally cedes, and, reel turn by reel turn, comes to hand. I hold it upside down with shaking wrists to disorient it, and dislodge the artificial fly from its jaw. Hook free, the fish is righted, vulpine snout to the sand, and rocked briefly like a small child in a bath, one hand behind the head and one hand at the tail, to circulate salt water through its gills. Revived in its element, it tightens, kicks, and heads for refuge, meeting a curtain of sand near the edge of the flat stirred up by two feeding spotted rays, and parting the murk opposite the tidal bore.

A rising orange sun laces its hazy light across the basin and my shadow clocks westward, a visible indication of a presence already sensed by the fish's schoolmates. Previously unnoticed, a short backhand cast away, the substantial congregation of fish arcs across the wales of sand, fleeing its birthright flat for a deeper corridor of water, reminding the angler that the ocean is an aggregate of all perceptions, not just his human ones.

The boy walks barefoot atop fine-grained sand that was once stone—thousands and thousands of years ago, millions of years ago, kalpas ago. Twelve years old. His toes dodge the snarled studs of remnant basalt uplift as he scours the ground for snails and shells, curves to eat. His brothers and sisters forage downshore from him, communal, businesslike. Breakfast was guona berries, cocoplum, wild derrie plucked from the bushes near his family's one-room house. The lucky ones find conchs, smash the horned pink shells with rocks and try not to slice their fingers on the shards as they peel the seething single-eyed creature from its hold.

Something scurrying or glistening with life: now and then he spots a live thing and crouches to pluck it from the sand. If it doesn't have claws or fins, he rinses it in a wave and pops it in his mouth; otherwise it's shoved into the darkness of the small burlap sack he'll bring for dinner. The water glides toward shore, then away, the tide falling from the mangrove shadows and lightly sketched tracks of hermit crabs, the glistening bag of a jellyfish brought in after two days of north wind, and, suddenly—this stops him in his tracks—the bleached skull of a long-dead hawksbill turtle, weathered to its orifices and distinctly human.

Despite his brothers' chiding, he carries it all afternoon: light to hold, but with a strange density to it. They merely want to touch it, perhaps toss it back and forth, but he fends them off, kicking sand at them like a lobster. He even refuses to relinquish it to his sisters while he dives a blue hole for lobsters; air bubbles peel off from the skull as he descends. Later, while warming himself by a fire built of coconut husks, he sprawls on his back and holds the skull to his eyes, peering through the sockets. Through these strange lenses, the evening sky is indigo. Later the horizon will bleed its strange ink upward and the heavens will darken thoroughly, Jupiter will appear precisely where he's staring, and the sky will fill with the constellations by which he's learned to navigate.

And that are up there even now, he comprehends, whether visible or not.

Roosting doves rustle in the shoreline sea grapes, two dogs scrap in the yard of the school from which the visiting British teacher recently fled just two months after arriving. The leathery scent of bougainvillea hangs over the road. The boy's mother has lit a lantern in the window of their house, the only structure in town that survived the last hurricane. Maybe tonight she'll tell the story again of how, when she was walking pregnant with him, a snake appeared in the road. Brother had a hoe slung over his shoulder, and he swung it on the snake. Whack. It lay there with its head cocked over. Just then you kicked inside me, and I touched my belly. That's why your left toe bends inward like it does. A birthmark.

He looks down at his odd track in the sand and stops to lean against the palm where he moors his boat. The fronds shift, though he feels no wind against his skin. He kneels and checks the rope. The smallest waves slurp at the hulls like clear tongues, recalling his thirst. Nearby the water's nervous with a small shoreward push: likely a school of the bony fish his neighbor sometimes nets. Save this tiny wake, the sea as far as he can see is planed and gray: an endless whetstone on which he hones his eyes.

Known Inhabitants

Who knows what causes the opening and closing of the
door?

—WANG WEI ·

As all good anglers know, one must from time to time shirk
a bit of responsibility in pursuit of one's quarry. After several months away, I was back in McLean's Town doing just that;
on assignment to write a where-to article for a glossy magazine,
a chalk fishing piece that would almost cover my plane ticket,
I found myself more drawn to the dangling thread of David's
story than to finding a catchy lead, and had wandered over to
his house in hopes of reconnecting.

David stood in his yard whittling a long pine branch into a
push-pole, peeling the bark from the wrist-thick wood with brisk
flicks of his forearm. Shavings sprayed with each machete stroke,
the blade bronzed by a matinal sun. I wasn't sure if he would
remember me, so I stood at the end of the driveway and yelled,
"Miller sends his greetings!" He looked up, cocked his head back
and forth like a bird, then lifted the brim of his ball cap from
his forehead, and pulled it back down with a nod, his long arms
hanging beside his lanky-strong frame like wind socks at dead
calm.

"Oh, yessir," he said, and set the knife and would-be poling
instrument atop an old skiff that rested upturned on two saw-
horses, waiting for repair.

I walked toward him and offered my hand.

·   ·   ·

IT TOOK A WHILE TO CARVE IN PAST THE SMALL TALK, BUT eventually David sorted through my scattershot questions and pointed north toward where he had grown up in a two-room house, bunking on the floor with his brothers, his sisters sharing a mattress in the next room, twelve kids all told and the slumber—what with all the arms and legs scratching bedbug bites—far from sound.

"Nights when I couldn't sleep," David said, his deep voice harmonizing momentarily with the guttural groan of the passing ferry's engine, "I would ask my father how we got here, so far from where he was born, on Eleuthera."

David breathed deep and looked up at the trees around the yard, the palms' fronds high-noon still. A good fishing morning, he offered, an aside not lost on my nerves.

Like many Bahamians of West African descent, David's father Samuel had been born a free man and roved the archipelago via sponging boat before landing at East End.

"Not much for stories, but he would tell it: 'You stop somewhere sponging and squat. Fall in love with a woman, squat.' He'd roust us in the dark with chores. 'Take the small boat up to Big Sound and walk the mud flats for shinies. A man coming to town soon will buy them.' Five dollars for a quart. Seven thousand to fill a jar. If we got home before he did we should dye and trim sponges, press the cured ones into bales. Tough work, but it beat sailing all day to Red Shank, oaring if the wind's not right."

One otherwise uneventful Thursday morning, Samuel Pinder, pastor of the McLean's Town church, would suffer a sudden stroke and die three days later on the Sabbath.

Not long after his father's funeral, David found himself teaching at the McLean's Town school—yet another visiting instructor had come, surveyed, taught for a few weeks, and, scrimshanking, left for parts unknown. Thus the school's finest student was tasked with giving rudimentary lessons until the next import arrived. One of his peers reminded him fondly of his mother. Her name was Nicey (*knee-sea*) and for a whole week in October she stayed home sick. Each day he fretted, and on Friday, instead of sending Nicey's homework with her sister, David sent a letter. A few months later sixteen-year-olds Nicey and David were married, the minister listing their ages in the official registry as eighteen, in adherence with Crown law.

"It was," he said, looking across the water at a horizon line obscured by humidity, "the year I got in love.

"I probably would have stayed a sponger's son. Who knows where I would have ended up? The wind would blow you one way one day, another way the next. We would hop from island to island on those sponging boats, but you couldn't make much money if you were black," he said, explaining that eight hundred sponges gathered by a black family would garner the same pay as five hundred sponges gathered by whites. "After a time all the sponge died. I think the Lord killed it off because it was being abused. Because we were being treated unfairly."

About the time the sponge rebounded, David, nineteen, was working on a hard-labor crew at a US missile-tracking site near Freetown. One mid-April evening a wealthy man from Palm Beach arrived in search of a hand.

An avid saltwater angler, Gil Drake had recently leased from the Crown a square-mile island across the channel from McLean's Town. Since purchasing land in the Bahamas in the late 1950s required royal connections, Drake's wife, who was of extremely high-test Philadelphia money to bankroll the purchase, called upon family friends Sir Henry and Lady Oaks, who shortly thereafter enlisted the queen. Since the island's moniker Crow Carrion wouldn't likely attract visitors and since Drake was ultimately hoping to build a fishing lodge on the north shore of the cay, he dubbed it Deep Water, and shortly thereafter, on the fourteenth day of April 1956, regarded a trio of young rock-lugging Bahamians, and approached the one who appeared the fittest of the three.

Did young David Pinder know it was the anniversary of Abraham Lincoln's assassination and the sinking of the *Titanic*? Did he sense something ominous in the air?

"I still count it as the luckiest day of my life," he said. We had made our way down his driveway to the water, where the tide was out. In the glaring distance a gull-chased fishing boat could be seen scribing a wide glare-cutting arc across the bay. "To have been chosen by Mr. Drake that day was a great privilege. I was barely earning four pounds a week at the missile site, small money. I was so happy he chose me over the other two.

"That was on Sunday. On Monday we were clearing mangroves so they could bring in a generator—he had hired two of my nephews as well—then later we put up a shed. This point, the Drakes lived on their boat, got their hands dirty just like us. We brought rocks in the dinghy across from McLean's Town, big chunks of rock and shoreline. Cracked them, mixed them into cement. Eventually Mr. Drake would hire a contractor from Palm Beach by the name of Charlie Couch who built the first cottage and lodge building. He shipped the materials down on a commercial fishing boat, but for now it was oaring over to camp loaded down with rock. The water almost over the gunwales."

Having foraged on the newly named Deep Water Cay for as long as he could remember, David was intimate with the terrain around the island Gil Drake had procured. As a youth he had harvested lobster from traps in nearby East End Creek, handlined Cubera from the underwater swale to the south of the island. He knew which blue holes were chock-full of craws, and when the tides were right to dive for them. But most important to his new employer: David had encountered plenty of bonefish.

"We hadn't been on the island for more than a week, when Mr. Drake's assistant comes to me with a very serious look on his face. 'David,' he says, 'Mr. Drake has something he needs to ask you. Immediately.'

"I know I haven't done a thing to upset anyone, but I assume there's some mess. I put down my machete, and walk over to Mr. Drake who's down at the water.

"'David, look,' he says, stone cold, pointing back toward town. 'Do you see the water rippling out there? A school of bonefish. You've seen them before?'

"Straightaway, I light up because I knew how to catch them with a hand-line—but I wonder what he wants with the bony things. So many better-eating fish. I'd seen them since my youngest days. Walking along the beaches, looking for something to eat, there were always schools around.

"Mr. Drake was mad for fishing. You could see him looking at the water every day, keeping his eyes peeled for fish. In between work shifts he would ask me to take him out in the boat. Pay was the same either way, fifty cents an hour. After two weeks he said he would hire me seven days a week, twelve months out of the year. Couple seasons later I was guiding full time."

Could this shore-foraging boy turned rock lugger ever have imagined that he would, decades down the line, be recognized as the head guide and cornerstone of one of the world's most fabled sporting lodges? Or that, a half century after Gil Drake first employed him, Bahamian prime minister Hubert Ingraham would visit Deep Water Cay Club to personally thank David Pinder for his indelible impact on the Bahamian economy and the sport of bonefishing, the activity upon which the Ministry of Tourism bases its faith?

"No sir, I never thought that far down the line," David said, kneeling in some tide-strewn turtle grass to lift a weathered

Kalik bottle from the wrack-line detritus of dry shells and flotsam. He held the bottle up to the sky and swooped it across that backdrop for a moment before shrugging his shoulders, as if to imply that it would be easier to account for the bottle's arrival here than to account for his and the bonefish's rise. He slid the bottle in his trouser pocket, knelt down again, and rinsed his hands.

The Old Feeling

What is man but his passion?

—ROBERT PENN WARREN

One of the first fishermen David guided, a childhood friend of Drake's son named Guy de la Valdene, arrived on Deep Water when the island was still choked with mangroves. Valdene has in the decades since authored several beloved books on hunting and angling, including *The Fragrance of Grass* and *Red Stag*, and recalls with fondness David's excellence in the early days of the club.

"When I was thirteen years old," he told me by phone, "I started traveling to Deep Water Cay with the Drakes. They lived in Palm Beach so it was just a short hop over. Gil Senior had leased the land from the Crown for ninety-nine years."

"From the get-go, David became the number-one guide," Valdene said with a tone of voice that balanced nostalgia and reverence, seemingly intrigued by my budding interest in David's life, the way a scholar might perk up at the mention of a long-forgotten classic. "David was superior intelligence-wise to the other guides. Head and shoulders above the rest. Strangest thing about David: he never used Polaroid sunglasses"—which, worn by nearly all anglers today, polarize the glare from the water's surface, and are considered essential to optic health and spotting fish.

"I don't know how long he fished without glasses, but he always saw the fish regardless. Very smart about how to approach the fish. Calm, moved the boat well. He was also a whiz at fixing engines, which seemed to break down every day. He moved fluidly from hauling rock to hacking mangroves to

33

catching lobsters to getting us into bonefish. There was a grace about him."

Having placed his youthful bare feet on nearly every square inch of the island before Gil Drake purchased it, having memorized the flats and their tides to the extent that plying them was instinctual, David flourished in his early guiding days. Because of his purview, he didn't need tide charts the way the Drakes did, and could lead them to spots that weren't shown on their nautical maps.

"Three or four months after the [Florida] Keys guys caught a record permit on the fly"—the permit, a flats-going member of the pompano family, is infamous for its fickle attitude toward flies—"we went to one of the flats on East End to look for a *world*-record permit on the fly. Eight-pound test, this big fucking thing took off! We took all the silly pictures, but we had no live-well because we'd gone out in the johnboat. Gil thought it was only twenty-five pounds, but it weighed twenty-seven, dried out. If we would have put it on the scale right away, it would have been the record by a few pounds, and of course we would have listed David as the guide. I think the picture is still up in the bar at the lodge."

When Valdene first started spending time at Deep Water Cay at age fourteen, there was nothing on the island: "And I mean there was *nothing*. We slept on a thirty-two-foot Nova Scotia called the *Magic*, and we helped build docks and clear ground every summer thereafter."

Virtually overnight the island became a destination for wealthy explorative anglers, due in part to its proximity to astoundingly fertile habitat—over 250 square miles of flats within a reasonable boat ride—and in part to its owner's friendship with *Field and Stream* fishing editor A. J. McClane, who profiled the outfit in his fabled magazine.

For the first few years, the lodge itself grew quite slowly, beam by beam, stair by stair, row of bricks by row of bricks, many of which were laid by David's hands. A little bungalow housed four anglers, Valdene recalled. "By the next year it accommodated eight, then twelve. But within three years, the lodge could comfortably host fourteen people."

A passage from a 1971 *Sports Illustrated* article by Coles Phinizy adds details to Valdene's sketch.

> By any name, the place doesn't interest most people. Which is good. The Deep Water Cay Club opened 12 years ago as a fishing resort and it is still that. Compared to the average tourist Casbah in the Bahamas, the club lacks a lot. It does not have a man-made, chlorinated swimming vat, or a cunning Buccaneer Bar, or a gambling casino, or a gift shop. The guests are welcome to use the backgammon board in the main lounge. At the desk a guest can buy monofilament and poppers, wigglers and squirmers, to catch fish and (sometimes) a brush to clean his teeth, but that's about the limit of it. The accommodations at the club are comfortable. The lizards that occasionally stray into the room are small and friendly. The food is simple but good; the drinks come from the best bottles and are cheap. The dinner conversation rarely drags and is always intriguing for those who dote on fish lore. The club has never advertised, but has depended simply on one satisfied customer telling another.

In large part, according to Valdene, said satisfaction stemmed from the fishing. "Very good for bonefish, but in those days it was all shrimp and spinning rods. There was very little fly-fishing. Al McClane did. I don't even think Gil's father or Gil did—or me for sure—for a long time."

.   .   .

POSITIONED CURIOUSLY IN THE EARLY DEEP WATER
dynamic was Gil Drake Jr., not for a moment the snotty kid of a
wealthy real state tycoon, but a true fish hawk who preferred the
company of Valdene and David to that of the lodge's moneyed
guests.

"In the early days the road from West End just stopped,"
Gil Junior recalled by phone from his home in Florida, where
he still makes a living as a guide. "We had to walk seven miles
down the limestone just to hit the dock in McLean's Town.
The kids would come up and pull the hair on my arms. They'd
never seen anything like it before, never seen a white guy.
Now of course they're totally self-sufficient, but back then
you couldn't really count on the locals doing anything without
supervision. I mean, they couldn't read a map, couldn't run
a boat without trashing the prop. But we got along well. We
were all using those cheap polarized glasses. Just about everyone who spent time on the water had cataracts. Not one of us
knew what he was doing. Famous guys like Al McClane, Joe
Brooks: nowadays they would be barely adequate casters, but
they looked the part."

Valdene, too, remembered the early fly-casting acolytes,
"the dudes in their khaki outfits: khaki shorts, khaki shirts,
everything was khaki. And all were kind of stodgy but very nice,
all very sweet people."

Then khaki-clad, if less than stodgy, a young Miller watched
dumbfounded as David, circa mid-1970s, first employed a fly
cast from the bow of a skiff.

"What's he doing?" Miller asked his father.

"He's cheating," his father said.

"What do you mean?"

"I mean, when we make a bad cast, we have to reel it all the way up and cast again. If he makes a bad cast, he just picks it up and wings it out."

Like most of the guests at the club, the Millers soon graduated to the more sporting means of fly casting for both its efficacy and its grace. They were among many who had never cast a fly rod but had, somewhere or other, seen one employed—the first loop of line sailing back and unfurling before being powered forward in a second unfurling loop—and wrongly assumed that the traveling line's fluidity would translate into an ease of aptitude.

Although twenty years had passed since Florida Keys captain Billy Smith landed the first fly-caught bonefish, saltwater fly tackle hadn't evolved much in the interim. Despite the elements' demands, rods were still fashioned largely from slow-moving fiberglass—a traditional, if slothy, material that serves well for tossing dainty dry flies on chalk streams in Pennsylvania for ten-inch trout, where an angler wading, say, the famed LeTort Spring Run might see a trout rise to take a natural mayfly in the shade of a willow, and be afforded the time to stop casting, change flies, perhaps light his pipe, then make a proper premeditated presentation of his fly to the steadily feeding fish. All of which is to say: neither angler nor prey, resting comfortably in its lie, is going anywhere in a hurry.

However, on the saltwater flats where middle-of-the-foodchain, ever-hunted targets such as bonefish don't loiter, anglers must be prepared to present flies instantly and instinctively, mirroring their quarry's modus operandi. ("Big bonefish coming fast at eleven o'clock," a guide might say, "ninety feet. Put it on his nose! Now!")

As a result, fiberglass and bamboo eventually gave way to speedier graphite, though even the early-generation rods of the mid-1970s responded too slowly to be considered effective, let alone enjoyable to wield. The necessities of a saltwater fly cast coupled with the prevailing elements (fifteen miles per hour is considered a light breeze on the flats) often turned experienced freshwater fly casters—accustomed to casting a rod weighing three ounces instead of one twice that weight—into first-rate floggers. One illustrative photo from the early fly-rodding era, accompanying a 1981 *Field and Stream* article about Deep Water Cay Club, shows author Ed Zern on the bow of David Pinder's skiff roughly two rod lengths from a tailing bonefish. Zern stands at attention, his casting arm tucked tight to his body, as if he were holding a Bible between his elbow and his ribs, the rod nearly as bulky as David's shaved-pine push-pole. Zern, one assumes, is about to enact a now-ancient casting model wherein anglers "tick-tocked" the rod back and forth between ten o'clock and two o'clock, twelve noon being straight overhead, on a metronome's rhythm—a model that the flats' demands, and David, quickly deemed worthless.

WHILE IT'S FORGIVABLE TO DRIFT OFF INTO THE HIGH LYRIC while imagining a backlit fly caster rhythmically zinging line back and forth inches from the water's surface, it's better to de-romanticize the fly rod, to recognize it for what it is: a tool someone fashioned to help one creature connect to another. Dame Juliana Berners, fifteenth-century Benedictine prioress and inventor of the sport, chose an alder limb and shaved it down to the proper weight. Five centuries and countless industry advancements later, I found after snapping my expensive graphite in a tumble on the way to the stream that a carefully selected willow branch would still suffice: knotted a monofilament leader to the tip of the branch, a likely fly to the end of the leader, and soon felt life tugging at the other end.

The contemporary, of course, necessitates complexity. Today's $900 graphite rods host custom cork grips at the base of which are seated machined reels containing Dacron backing, synthetic fly line, and monofilament leader. Knots like slip-, Albright, and nail connect these lines, which taper from a butt end like spaghetti to a working end of angel hair. To the end of the clear leader, via blood knot, a two-foot section of tippet testing ten or twelve pounds is tied, and to the end of the tippet a bonefish fly is cinched.

Like language, the artificial fly is a brutal approximation.

The impressionist flytier wraps some chicken rump feathers and chopped-up rabbit fur dyed mauve to the shank of a stainless steel hook, adding two small black plastic bulbs meant to mimic a crab's eyes; the realist, however, scissors a hunk of brown carpet into a disk, threads it to the hook's shank, and glues it there with two strips of white leather, razor-cut to look like claws, then epoxies a piece of real crab shell to the abdomen, to achieve the texture of the natural. No matter how impressionistic or realistic, the fly evidences the unbridgeable distance between expression and experience.

While anglers and flytiers argue the merits of their patterns like stumping politicians, most bonefish guides scoff at a well-catalogued box of fly patterns—"It's not the arrow, it's the archer," they say.

In such terms, the bow is the fly rod, and the rod, if we're fishing during the early 1960s, is bamboo, likely made in upstate New York with cane imported from the Bay of Tonkin, the cork from Asia, too. In the mid- to late seventies, the rod is fiberglass and fashioned in San Francisco. Thenceforth the angler likely wields lighter and stronger graphite pressed and fused together in the Pacific Northwest, new models of rods every year, like fashion lines. The same folks who engineer cassette tapes manufactured the floating line in Michigan. The fly's steel hook point has been honed by a laser in parts unknown. The serpentine aluminum guides, line keepers running incrementally along the length of the rod, are aluminum from a refinery in Illinois. The hen feathers trailing off the fly come from an Ohio farm that breeds fowl to produce high-grade hackle, the fur dubbing from a rabbit trapped and killed by a young boy in Kentucky who sells his pelts per dozen to a man from Lexington who sells them by the gross to a company named Wapsi out of Arkansas. Maybe the angler hand-tied the fly, maybe he ordered it from a Montana-based company that shops out its labor to factories in Costa Rica and Thailand.

All this is to say that no matter how isolated the flats angler appears or thinks herself (and clearly she searches for some pleas-ant desolation as she stalks fish barefoot, adjacent to the shore of an unnamed Caribbean cay whose sole inhabitants since time immemorial have been cormorants and frigate birds), when the hooked bonefish accelerates like a gazelle fleeing a cheetah, and the integrity of five knots is tested, along with the rod's backbone, along with the reel's oiled clutch—when the line tightens, a dozen seemingly disparate worlds fuse with a flourish, and she feels, as Hemingway's Nick Adams felt upon spotting a long-desired trout from a high north woods riverbank, "all the old feeling."

This old feeling is far, far older than we can imagine. And yet we touch it through the new.

THAT DAVID HAD NEVER CAST A FLY ROD PRIOR TO HIS employer's arrival was perhaps to his advantage; because the former had never learned that it was "improper" to bring the fly rod past two o'clock on the back-cast, he was able to perform the mechanics of the hand-lining cast with just the line, hook, and sinker.

"You work harder at what you love," David explained to me one evening as a cumulus at the foot of the southern sky caught the falling sun like a baseball. I was trying to listen intently to his wellspring of backstory but found myself repeatedly drawn to the memory of a huge bonefish, my biggest to date, that I had hooked earlier in the day and lost, after a two-hundred-yard run, on a barnacled mangrove stem—that twenty-second connection to a ten-pounder, before the tippet gave way, the briefest of affairs, most clinical of severances.

David waited for me to return, then continued.

"I was always the last guide to leave the lodge. Some nights the Drakes would leave a fly rod on the dock and I would go on the beach and practice with it after work was done. I had their permission. I couldn't do much with it, but they couldn't do much, either. It was still a foreign object back then. I believe it was a cane rod, bamboo, but it could have been fiberglass as well. Whippy as a skate's tail. Anyway. I got to thinking about our old coffee cans with fishing line wrapped around them, the way we used to hand-line—you had to use a lot of arm to get that hook and sinker going, so that their weight would carry out the line. About then I started heaving with that fly rod. Big wide-open looped casts, way more line than those other boys were using. It wasn't pretty at first, but it was something."

By opening up the cast's loop, and dropping the rod almost parallel to the water, David was able to create more fulcrum, thus momentum, thus line speed, and thus conquer the element that had been besting American sports since they first arrived on the bonefish flats: the wind.

A saltwater angler's most plaguing bane, wind flummoxes from all four directions, alternately hampering both back-cast and forward cast. Say the angler stands on the bow of a skiff in a fifteen-mile-per-hour headwind: the wind will accommodatingly sling his back-cast out at the speed of sound, but will stunt the forward cast or otherwise urge it toward unintended locales. A tailwind, on the other hand, forces the angler to initiate the back-cast with extra chutzpah so that the line's loop unfurls; thus the forward cast comes rocketing uncontrolled past the angler, who, if he's had a brass-eyed fly whack him in the back of the neck a time or two, knows to duck. If a wind comes across the body, both angler and guide find themselves in high dudgeon: again the back-cast snaps to perfect planed-out attention, but the forward cast resembles a willow branch in a tornado. Grunts and body English don't help one "play the wind" but are nonetheless frequently employed. At the back of the skiff, the guide removes his hat and kneels, either in supplication or to avoid puncture.

"Most of the guests were pretty bad," David said of the early days. "I used to wear an old baggy jacket so that when they would hit me on their back-cast, the flies would go into the jacket instead of my skin. The thing was full of holes. Do they hit you with the flies up north?"

Pleased that he had acknowledged, for the first time, our shared profession, I nodded with exuberance: *Oh, do they.*

"One time a guest was on the boat with his young son," David said. "He had the hardest time spotting the fish. This can be frustrating but sometimes it helps because the client doesn't get too riled up, he just does what he's told: fifty feet, three o'clock. Finally the man sees a big bonefish coming toward us and he winds up, winds up, and sticks the fly right in his son's thigh! The man's still excited, so he's whipping the line around, thinking he's just tangled around himself. But the son is screaming, 'Dad, it's in me! It's in me!'"

David watched the guests from the back of the skiff, unnerved by the approaching fish, and learned what inhibited his clients' febrile casts. Mostly not enough power, going ten-to-two, ten-to-two, restricting the arm's strength and the line's ability to power the rod. His mechanical casting epiphany equaled distance, and casting distance earned him credibility with the guests. What followed, as bonefish became an industry, far eclipsed credibility:

"There were some great guides at Deep Water Cay," Valdene told me, "but for decades, David Pinder was famous."

From the lips of the man poling the Sea-Squid through a stiff northeaster, a sound squeaks forth—something he almost says but doesn't. His bantering clients hush and turn to their guide, who weighs what he may have seen against hours of piscine vacancy, against the assurance of a timely arrival at the dock, against his better interests.

At the bow on the casting platform stands his client, British guest of his employer and potential investor at the lodge, gazing like someone who might suddenly fall prey to a narcoleptic episode.

Planting the edge of the push-pole starboard, inclining against the skiff's momentum, the man says he might, he's not sure, have seen a wake in the cove. Explaining that the fish's tail will look like a mangrove leaf, he urges the Brit not to blink. The man has yet to see an actual fish but the tide is slipping out and revealing the bottom's subtle sags and crab domes, several half-dollar-size indentations in the muck made by a feeding fish's attempts to dislodge prey. A trail of these half-dollars leads to the inlet.

The lodge owner perks up from his seat on the dunnage box and whispers the Brit to attention. Be ready. I can tell by his tone.

The man points his push-pole over the Brit's left shoulder. Tailing fish, he says. You see the leaf pointing sideways? A tail.

The Brit says he sees the fish, but his voice belies his uncertainty.

Coming straight over the skiff's transom, the wind wants to sail the boat with the man's billowed shirt for a jib away from the cay, but he pins the pole port, deep in the soft seafloor. That he holds his ground for thirty, forty seconds, without so much as bumping the pole on the skiff's fiberglass sidewall, is a feat the lodge owner will later gush over.

From somewhere inside the oily green leaves a catbird mews. On his fourth try, the Brit lands the fly in the wheelhouse.

Whatever you do, the lodge owner intones, don't move the rod tip on the take again or you'll pull the fly out of the fish's mouth. You can't let the right hand know what the left hand is doing.

Though neither of his guests perceives any indication as to why, the man, from his slightly higher vantage, commands the Brit to set the hook.

Somehow the Brit manages to heed the voice in each ear, keeping his right wrist rigid while pulling tight a yard of line with his left. As the rod flinches and bucks with animal energy as the fish leaves the mangroves in its wake, the lodge owner curses at his guest to clear the line: Watch your shoelaces, goddammit! That's why we go barefoot.

With the loose line spooled to the reel, the Brit puts the buzzing Hardy to his ear and declares the fish tallied.

Not on the board quite yet, the lodge owner chides. Still have to land it.

Crown law, Drake, Crown law. A solid hookup goes down in the book.

Running, the fish scribes a wide parabola on the flat, fifty yards west by southwest, then sixty yards south by southeast, stopping to breach not far from where it first felt the hook. The Brit's line, beset with slack, lolls in the wind.

Gather the line, the man says, poling the boat away from the fish to tighten the surplus lest the fish spit the hook.

The Brit switches the rod to his left hand, so that he can reel with his dominant right, and cranks with abandon like a man vigorously scrambling an egg in a bowl, regaining connection with the fish momentarily before stopping to take a breath. During this inaction, the fish feels the line pressure falter and uses its brief loose leash to weave back into the mangroves. He heaves to pull the fish back. The rod blank creaks. Then he groans and deflates, piling atop his knees on the casting platform.

Give some slack, the man says, and he might come out yet.

Like stitches bursting at a seam, small bright flicks of water appear at the surface as the fish braids its way through the sub-

merged roots. The Brit watches, stands, and with a grunt of reso-
lution bows the rod again and yanks. The clear leader snaps with
an audible crack, and he stumbles backward off the casting deck;
simultaneously the rod recoils, straightens briefly overhead, clocks
forward with uncontrolled fulcrum momentum and slams, just as
he regains balance, onto the bow.

The shattered fiberglass hangs together at the ferrule by a few
fibers, a broken antenna.

No one says a thing. A catbird lifts from the mangroves, rows
a few strokes upwind, then turns tail. Someone curses, someone
laughs. Then the lodge owner lifts the cooler lid with his toe and
hands a beer to the Brit, who cracks it and takes a quick triple
swallow, insisting, as he wipes foam from his lips, that he'll pay to
have to have the rod replaced. The lodge owner will hear none of
it. The beer, though, he jokes, will cost three hundred American.

The men laugh—the incident has not vitiated the afternoon but emblazoned it in memory. They reenact the moment
with comic gestures. Perhaps the potential investment, all but
embalmed at lunchtime after nearly three days of angling futility,
now possesses at least a pulse.

Staring from his perch atop the boat's motor at the mangrove warrens into which the bonefish disappeared, the man reck-
ons that the fish might yet be lingering: the snapped line looped
around a mangrove shoot, attempting to worry the hook out of its
mouth. True, the other guides are home with their second glass of
Green Seed in hand, but on a slim day like this, it is worth a look.

The man begs pardon and, jumping down into the water from
the transom, asks his employer to hold this stake. Quick glance
before we go, he says.

Not on my account, the Brit insists. I had my fair shot.

But the man is already over the transom, making for the cay.
He takes several fleet steps on the firm bottom before a layer of

muck elasticizes his strides, then he dives in and front-crawls the last ten yards to shore. As he surfaces, two previously unseen brown pelicans lift ponderously out of the mangroves and bank away on the wind.

Not far into the maze of gray roots, the man sees his favored pink fly betraying the fish's camouflage. Strung taut between the hook and the shoot around which it was wound, a yard of fifteen-pound-test monofilament tippet shines. Most fish would have fled at his footfalls, but this gorged seven-pounder merely wallows on its back as the man nears, eyeing his approach submissively through its nictitating membrane. With his right hand the man clasps the fish behind the gills; his left hand snaps the shoot off at its base.

. . .

THE ROTUND THING LIES GASPING ON THE FLOOR OF THE BOAT, still attached to the mangrove, and the lodge owner asks to have a look inside the distended belly.

A swift flick with the fillet knife from the anus to the gills: the man is quick to dispatch since the act insures the fish will feed his family later tonight. He peels out the cauly strings of the intestines, the red inner workings, and proffers the stretched bag of the stomach, which he slits open with the tip of the blade: out spills a partially digested shrimp, a small blue crab missing one of its claws, a schoolmaster, and a beet-red urchin—all of which he tosses without further regard over his shoulder and into the water.

This curious handful of food: the man's memory of it, the details precise, unflinching, will persist against the wash of time.

From behind them, with the noise of heavy rain, a barracuda surfaces and with three open-mawed swipes clears the water of the chum. Then before the water settles, before the men can so much as remark, the barracuda rockets toward the boat on the edge of its tail, chased by a shark that, with a thump off the hull, wheels and catches the 'cuda: the hunter turned hunted vanishing in the ten-foot lemon's bloody stranglehold.

The man chokes the engine twice and lets it idle for a moment, then revs the throttle and runs the skiff onto a plane.

Southerly

One must work to achieve enlightenment and then
return to the common world.

—BASHO

Meko was going to teach me how to pole a skiff—that
was the notion, anyway. A southerly snapped the flags
straight, though, and the waves in the channel lapped on themselves in frothy lines. Late day, dead low tide: the sand from
which the water had recently receded shining like billowing
silk. Hands full of rigged rods, a backpack of tackle strung over
my shoulder, I bumbled down to the docks where a few guides
lingered after a long day's work, hosing down their boats, scrub-
bing the chines free of grime.

"What's all the gear for?" Meko called, wringing out a
sponge. "I thought you were driving and I was fishing!"

"I wasn't sure, with all this—" I pointed up at the rough-
housing palms.

"You know what they say about the wind," said a tall mus-
tached guide I hadn't met. He took a toothpick from his mouth
and shot hose water at Meko's feet. "It blows."

"You'll have to forgive my uncle William," Meko said, putting a hard-bristled brush to the floor of his boat. "He was out
with the governor today so he's a little chippy."

Later I would learn that a high-ranking elected official from
the South was indeed visiting the lodge—also that William
Pinder was one of David's sons—but for the time being I just
nodded, like I was in the know.

"Up to the Cross Cays," William said. "Fussy fish.
Spooked every fish we saw except the mudding ones. Fit,

though. Man, you could pole a skiff through a puddle with him."

"Up to Big Sound, maybe?" Meko asked.

"Worth a look tomorrow afternoon on the flood," William said, motioning for Meko to throw him the brush. "You've got the governor tomorrow. Everybody wants to fish with Meko."

I hung my feet over the edge of the dock and listened to a third guide—baby faced, twenty years old, I guessed—seated behind the silver steering wheel of his unwashed skiff, complain animatedly about how the veterans always got more experienced clients, thus handicapping the youth. *How am I supposed to find a fish for a guy who can't cast two pole lengths?* Meko nodded, acknowledging, I assumed, the youth's soliloquy as the clichéd lament of an angler who could find fish but lacked the ability to communicate with nuance and thus establish a trusting client base. Once the young guide had motored off to the gas tanks, Meko and William began to recount the day's trips in detail.

Always a bit therapeutic in nature, these postguiding exchanges usually contained a bit of truth, a dose of braggadocio, a jab at a client's ineptitude or ambivalence, and maybe even an element of friendly trickery—were the bonefish truly spooky in the Cross Cays, for instance, or was William simply reporting as much so he could have the flat to himself tomorrow? In Montana, anyway, I might buy a fellow guide a drink to grease the proverbial wheels, but the top-shelf stuff was attainable solely through the barter system: tell me something true, and I'll do the same for you.

I reflected on how, to some extent, my own guiding had become, after over a decade of work, largely transactional. True, my days rowing the boat helped supplement the threadbare living I made as a poet and a teacher, but my passion for fishing— which I had loved to distraction since adolescence, even when pretty young women complicated the equation—had devolved

into the occupational. My brief conversations with David had
led me to believe that down here, anyway, the occupation of
guiding was considered a vocation. *Vocari*, I remembered from
an old poem. *To be called.*

FORETOLD BY WING-WHISTLE, A TIGHT FLOCK OF
greenshanks spilled over the boat and disappeared up the bight,
vagrants in the islands. We motored east in the gradually falling
light into the backcountry in search of calmer poling conditions,
but also so that Meko, already on a busman's holiday of sorts,
could scout a flat he hadn't fished in weeks. The spot, he told me,
was frequented by a few very large specimens, and he was hoping to get the governor on a double-digit bonefish the following
day. He couldn't show it to me, of course; he would have to drop
me off on the south side of the island after the poling lesson.

"You can fish your way back as the tide comes in," he said,
cutting the motor. "About a mile to the lodge from where I'll leave
you. Just keep moving toward the sun and you'll be there long
before dark. David's planning to meet you after supper." I understood his instructions not only as a test, but also as a small gesture of trust. I was a freshwater guide from somewhere up north,
but could I walk a straight line without getting lost, find a bonefish without someone holding my hand? Meko reckoned I could.
"When I come to Montana someday, you can show me a spot."

Once up on the skiff's poling platform, I crouched, closer to
kneeling than standing, certain I would topple, the foot of the
push-pole reaching to the sand and grinding against a staghead.
Vertiginous or not, I felt as if I were looking at the flats for the
first time: I saw *into* the small tidal lagoon ensconced in waist-
high mangroves, and noted not only the seafloor's subtle gains in
elevation, but the turtle grass, slack as a grounded kite, unbent by
tide; I noted what was stationary, a small midden of conchs at the

periphery, as opposed to moving, a fringed filefish named by an ichthyologist, I guessed, who hoped his mouth would experience in the saying of its name the same richness his eyes beheld.

"We're drifting too close, man," Meko said from the bow. He wasn't holding a rod, perhaps indicating his level of confidence in my poling abilities. "Back us off from the trees."

Weighing nearly a ton all told, the boat—with motor, gas, coolers, and humans—leaned back against my pose. I muscled against the angle of the pole and we slid away from the bank.

"Now try to hold us here," he said. "Put the pole on the other side. But swing it around behind you or you'll knock your guest in the water. Yep, like that."

I felt as if I'd been asked to push a stalled truck across an icy parking lot, then, as soon as it gained some momentum, to run around the rig and stop its movement. For several minutes, not without the drollery of a driver's education class, as the muscles in my arms burned from shoulder to fingertip, I attempted to steer the boat as Meko directed. I moved the boat with all the fluidity of a Fifth Avenue rush-hour taxi. Finally, after I ran the boat aground and almost stumbled from the platform, I asked Meko how I was doing, just to test his temperament. The guide's perpetual dilemma: candor or diplomacy.

"I think it's pretty windy to learn," he said. "You've got just enough good light to fish your way back to the lodge." He dug into his shirt pocket and handed me a small reddish-brown fly that he said would match the crop of weeds that congregated at the island's outer edge. "And I've got some fish to find before dinner."

FROM THE SOUTHEAST TIP OF DEEP WATER CAY, I WORKED my way west. The wind had settled like an infant finally exhausted from fussing, and the air smelled inexplicably of cinnamon—drying seaweed, I ventured. Earlier in the week, I had stepped accidentally on a man-of-war, exploding the glossy bag's toxins on my calf, and when the waves sloshed against my right leg, the tight skin above my ankle stung smartly. Pain notwithstanding, it felt good to be in the body. For as far south as I could see and begin to fathom, the ocean unfolded over my left shoulder like a limitless blue page, and as I walked a small strip of land in my sandals with no boat or house or human in sight, Gil Drake's brilliant foresight struck me: he had staked his island claim at the dead end of a rutted road, as far as he could get from humanity.

An imaginary glimpse into the Drake family bank account allowed the momentary worry of my monetary difficulties to steal in. I tried to walk it off. I had long ago, perhaps adolescently, permanently applied the Thoreauvian notion of success—only if "I shall have left myself behind"—to angling journeys. My fear struck me as a fire whose heat was increased as I fed it with the tinder of more worry. If I left its proximity, it might eventually die out. "Be where you are," my wife is fond of saying before a trip. If trekking the southern shore of a remote island wasn't going to help, nothing ever was.

I'd walked a good way before I saw a bonefish oceanside, and it disappeared in the window of a wave before I could cast. I kept on, though, the salience of that single fish fueling my hopes. Not soon, at the threshold between the ocean and a small backwater: commotion, the surface breaking and resettling audibly like a pool at the base of a cistern into which a handful of coins has been thrown. Instinctively I thought bonefish, but it was simply a needlefish fleeing a barracuda with what could have been mistaken for glee. I took a few strides and the corner of my eye caught something: beneath no more than a foot of water, in light that was tawny, fibrous, swam a single tailing bone.

Composed as a midocean wave, the fish moved elliptically around the lagoon, pausing to feed every few yards. Based on the fish's vulnerability and the placidity of the water, I figured I would get one shot. At most. It had made two laps before I could position myself on my knees, looking into the sun so that my shadow stretched away from my quarry, and ready my line for a presentation. I waited until the fish tipped down to tail, then unfurled my cast—loop, line, leader, tippet, fly—which landed a good yard short.

I couldn't do anything but sit the fly and hope the fish conscribed another grave circle. Four times it fed—I'm tempted to say it moved counterclockwise, but what transpires in such moments occurs in direct opposition to second hands and horizontal time—showing the full fork of its tail, and when I gauged it within a rod length of my fly, I gave the line a trigger strip. The water boiled and the line came tight. I set the hook and stood, just in time to see the unhooked bonefish bolt from the lagoon—the forgotten needlefish had stolen in to grab my fly, and friskily flipped it free. I threw my hands up in the air, a pulpiteer without a congregation.

By the time I reached the docks it was dusk, and David had been waiting. The tide was in, the mangroves' leaves were treading water, and a ruler-length barracuda milled around the dock pilings making its presence known to a checkered puffer and a few yellowfin mojarra that darted over the silty bottom. I made the always-precarious step from boat to dock, the width of the water beneath me widening slightly, and greeted David with an apology.

"No sir," he replied with an extended hand. "If you've been fishing, late isn't late."

I told him in detail about stalking the penned-up bonefish and the conspiring needlefish, that iniquitous creature.

"I remember a time that Joe Brooks," David said, crossing his long legs, "you know, the writer?"

"Of course," I said, neglecting to mention that I had read, the winter before I started guiding, every book on fishing that Brooks had penned. Back then I covered women's hockey for the *Idaho Statesman,* and spent my afternoons devouring the Boise Public Library's impressive outdoor writing section, the library couches far more comfortable than the half-deflated air mattress on which I spent my nights. "He was prolific."

"Well, I would guess late sixties, he came down to do an article on the lodge," David said. "We looked all week for a permit that he could put on the cover of the magazine. Finally we're out by Brush Cay and we spot what we think is a big permit, maybe a record, and Brooks puts a cast on the fish, and the fish takes. A mutton snapper, my friend!"

"What happened?"

"I don't think it made the cover shot," David said, uncrossing his legs and straightening the pleats of his starched khakis. "You go looking for this, the ocean gives you that."

I asked if he remembered anything else about Brooks's visit.

"On the last day, we found a group of bonefish so big you could barely see the flat. Probably a thousand fish. Mr. Drake had been touting me all week but the conditions had been rough. Big tides. Mr. Drake would say, 'David can spot a fish a half a mile away, he can hear a leaf turn at a hundred yards.' So I had confidence, but Brooks thought his friend was full of hot air.

"On that flood tide, though, we caught so many fish Brooks burned the gears out on two reels. He was tickled, wanted some pictures of me for his article, so I waited around the kitchen for an hour while the men had cocktails."

I pictured David standing behind the swinging case doors backed by a few white-bloused waitresses as Drake and Brooks, showered, clean-shaven perhaps, sat sipping from sweaty tumblers under the baking ceiling boards of the lodge's screened-in porch.

"Back then no guides were allowed in the dining room, but

the ferry was waiting to take me across the channel and dinner was ready. So I peeked my head in"—I imagined the door
opening shyly, its hinges whining like a catbird's call—"and said,
'Excuse me, sir, but . . .'

"Mr. Drake spun around so red in the face, he couldn't even
speak. He slammed his glass down, shook his head, and turned
away.

"It was the only time—" David said, checking his story,
his poise slightly betraying his poignant memory of the night,
forty-some years prior, when his place in the club dynamic was
made clearer to him.

Headed toward the setting sun, a lobster boat moved loudly
through the channel. A wave folded in beneath our feet and var-
nished the black stones under the dock. Above us, in darkening
branches, a dove cooed, then ceased its cooing, and, reminded
of a poem, I wasn't quite sure which I liked better: its song or
the quiet just after.

Through the Guide's Eyes

For the decidedly mythic life, there are
no minor gods.

—GASTON BACHELARD

My professor lit his pipe, puffed vigorously several times, then sighed with resignation: "So you're gonna be a whore, huh?"
Spring of sophomore year at my little Midwestern college, and under the guise of needing extra help on a paper that attempted to dovetail Turgenev's *Sportsman's Sketches* and serfdom's end in Russia, I had scheduled a tutorial with my beloved Russian-history professor, Penrose. Penrose had taught college for a quarter century and his lectures lit up the classroom, but what endeared him to me was that he built wooden MacKenzie boats, towed them each summer to the Clark Fork and Big Hole Rivers of his native Montana, and fished the faculty meetings he so despised back into the nothingness that had begat them. I was so amped to tell him my summer plans that I skipped right past Czar Nicholas and cut to the quick: I planned to go west permanently, to find a job guiding fly-fishing trips in Montana.

"It's whoring," he repeated, striking his lighter again.

Penrose understood my passion for fishing, even fed it; the previous summer he had taught me to navigate a drift boat, and he regularly passed down used fishing gear to me. But he didn't temper his lecture to accommodate my wide-eyed, white-faced reaction. A whore, he went on to say, becomes your friend for money. A whore sells previously secret and sometimes sacred experiences. A whore does not discriminate between deserving and undeserving clientele. A whore allows experience to be purchased. A whore compromises constantly for the almighty buck. And so on.

Throttled, I sat in silence across from my mentor, who could quote liberally from every Chekhov play, knew Turgenev's peasants and serfs by chapter and scene, but whom I trusted largely because he smoked a pipe. Men who smoked pipes mulled things over, and mullers possessed opinions worth listening to. Years later I would muse on his notion of guiding as whoring, wondering what type of employment didn't constitute some kind of prostitution, questioning if the oldest profession in the world wasn't also the most honest. But presently I was certain as cement that if I didn't go Montana to guide I would spend another listless summer living in my parents' basement, waking late to play driveway basketball all afternoon with equally delinquent high school friends, knocking off only to drink beers on our parents' porches and make plans for further boozing after showers and freeloaded dinners at home.

I went west.

What does a map of Montana and its rivers look like to the young angler who, a day prior, was navigating Chicago's man-made canyons, but now stands sipping camp stove–made coffee at the tailgate of his used pickup truck near the mouth of the mighty Madison River? The brown swaths of wilderness land, the green swatches of public forest, the blue pupil-size dots that stand for high mountain lakes from which vein-like blue lines curl down and through drainages—unfolded on the pickup's hood, the map looks like a wide doorway, each winding body of water a hallway leading to some room even more stunning than the last.

JEWEL-CLEAR, HIGH MONTANA SKY. SKIFT OF SNOW ON THE road shoulder and on the boughs of hillside pines lit so sharply by the southerly sun their distant needles appear countable. On my way from Bozeman to Boise in pursuit of a young woman's favor, I stopped for a leg stretch in the village of Sheridan, Montana, on the edge of which stood a small red barn of a building, redder for the snow, called Harman's Fly Shop. There was no sign in the window, but I figured that any fly shop well lit on a frigid December day was my kind of fly shop.

The owner, a gruff gray-bearded man whose name I'd heard was Tom, sat at his fly-tying desk working on a traditional woven-body George Grant Creeper, a ridiculously arduous fly to tie, an hour-long engagement to be sure. His German shorthairs shared a Filson dog bed and rose briefly from their slumber to growl at me.

"Jaeger! Packer!" Tom barked back. "Shut the hell up. First customer in days and you growl?"

"I don't guess you're filling many fly bins with those woven-body Creepers," I said, wanting him to note my knowledge of his craft.

"We're not trying to get rich here," he said, "just keep people happy."

There isn't much to do in a winter fly shop but bullshit, so after introducing myself I rambled about the Ruby River, which I'd fished during dizzying caddis hatches the previous two summers, and the Beaverhead, which I had learned to love for its sight fishing and tackle-humbling big browns, and my favored Big Hole, where Penrose had schooled me in the art of rowing. Tom lifted his gray eyebrows over his reading glasses now and then to show me he was listening, but mostly he focused on his fly. After a while, figuring I'd bored him, I thanked him for his time, bought a hat, and decided to get back on the road. The door chime sounded as I stepped out into the cold.

I leaned back in.

"Uh, Tom. I was just thinking. You wouldn't happen to be looking for an apprentice this summer? A guide? I've got some experience."

Tom looked up from lacquering the ribbed abdomen of his creation.

"You know, it's funny you should ask. Just today my head guide told me he was hanging up his oars for a contracting job. Yesterday the next guy on the totem told me he was due for shoulder surgery, could only work wade trips. So, yeah, as it so happens, I *am* looking for a guide. You passed the interview. Show up here May fifteenth with a boat trailered to that truck outside and we'll get you started."

After nagging him by phone three times a week throughout the winter, I started working for Tom the following June. It was the summer of flat truck tires and stripped trailer bearings fixed by Tom, the summer of countless wildfires and marginal tips, the summer Tom's wife left him for the town preacher, the summer that initiated his heavyweight bout with depression, a fifteen-round fight that would end with his suicide late in the summer of 2013.

I RENTED A $250-A-MONTH CABIN ALONG THE JEFFERSON River that summer. Each day I gassed up the truck in Twin Bridges (population 373) for a buck twenty-five per gallon, bought a couple of fifty-cent doughnuts for breakfast, washed them down with fifty-cent swill coffee, then blazed up the road to Harman's Fly Shop, where I picked up my lunch and clients for the day. This was 1998, or '97. I made $190 a day, plus tips. My sole expenses: fuel, breakfast, dinner, and beer, the last of which clients often left by the caseload in my cooler. I worked early June through mid-October, roughly 125 days all told, and saved enough money to pay off my Stafford college loan in one fell swoop.

For a few years, the influx of seasonal money makes a young guide sailor-rich enough to ignore any moral objections he might have to "whoring out" his good fishing holes, to dealing with arrogant sports, logging long hours in thunderstorms, high winds, extreme heat, and anything else the natural world throws at him. No one who is even remotely bothered by hard physical labor will last too long rowing a boat, or loading coolers and anchors, or shipping oars. The young guide relishes, is vaguely addicted to, driving home physically spent, having twice earned the beer he sips as his boat-towing truck slides past the last few twilit ranch hands moving irrigation pipe. He might even romanticize himself as a rancher of sorts, a trout-cowboy living quasi off the land on the fringes of society. A few years later, by the time his conscience catches up with him, or he herniates a disk in his back, and a yearning for "normalcy" or "security" strikes him, it's quite possibly too late for either.

After a couple of seasons I received a fellowship offer to study poetry writing in graduate school, accepted it, and switched to guiding on my summers off. I thought I would eventually be lured away by a teaching job, forced to sell my boat and move on entirely. But even after engaging a couple of these gigs full time, I found what my adolescent hero Norman Maclean called "the recipe for schizophrenia"—life split between the classroom and the woods—all too alluring. In the following years guiding helped my family subsist, but its fragmentary role only increased the dissonance in my life—it was, in other words, a far cry from the deepened way of engagement I later discovered in David's life.

Other guides I broke in with moved on to sell insurance or rep outdoor gear, but a few who later received MBAs or law degrees still guide forty days each year. True outliers, they were

feral for too long to give up their freedom cold turkey; they realized, after a decade on the oars, that they were mostly guiding
a return clientele made up of kindred spirits, enjoyable folks
whose own freedom and instincts may have been stunted in the
climb toward worldly success.

   To tell it plainly if paradoxically, guiding is a business based
on relationships. A guide and his clients play for the same team,
and the better the morale, the better the team performs. Florida Keys guides are a notoriously nasty, hypercritical bunch of
coaches, but even they will crack jokes to cut the tension on
the boat. Most Bahamian guides are deferential and happy to
accept fault when a fish isn't taken, but plenty stand at the ready
to cast blame on the angler and point out deficiencies. During
lulls in the action, some steelhead guides in British Columbia
use small talk—*Where are you from? Sure, Amherst. I have a
good friend who lives up there and teaches at the college*—while
others chew snuff and smoke copious amounts of homegrown
grass. In the Yucatan a Mayan permit guide might pole his boat
in silence all day until he sees "feeesh! Twelve o'clock! Permit!
Beeeg permit!"

   If the transaction is to proceed efficaciously, an interesting
inversion of power must occur: the paying client must submit
to the authority of the guide he or she has hired. To guide is to
trade one's set of skills and knowledge for a client's inferior set,
to relinquish the traditional means but not the hoped-for outcome, to become an extremely intuitive horse leading both rider
and himself to water. The savvy client comprehends this complicated dynamic. The arrogant sport, the one who can't eschew
the type-A mentality that might have put him in the position to
afford the trip, is often stymied.

   Ever adaptive, the best guides sense this, just as they sense
their clients' level of skill, interest, humor, candor, and thickness
of skin, and alter tactics and instruction accordingly. Occupying

a heightened awareness, seeing and intuiting what most clients cannot, spotting the raindrop-size rise form a huge trout makes at two hundred yards, negotiating a drift boat through a Class III plunge pool rapid while netting a leaping fish, predicting the precise moment of increased humidity at 2:37 in the afternoon when a dense hatch of mayflies will occur, the veteran is often asked, "How on earth did you do that? How did you know that was going to happen?"

Understandably the question leads some fishing guides to develop a hero complex. It's why they're so easily spotted at bars or on the dock—they possess an air of accomplishment, of having *done something*. It may have only been getting a rube of an angler into his first fish, or simply putting up with and not punching an unbearable client—but it was something.

And yet most days, the affections end at the boat ramp when gillie and sport part ways. Perhaps the two exchange contact information—"If you're ever in San Francisco!"—or make plans to fish again next year—"You should come for the salmon-fly hatch in early June, it's epic!" Generally there is some type of gratuity dispersed, a Benjamin or two sneaked into a handshake. Occasionally, though, sometimes due to arduous or fortuitous circumstances or sometimes inexplicably instant kinship, a bond is forged between guide and client that transcends the business transaction and moves them into the rarified realm of friendship.

When Jefferson Miller stepped into my truck in September of 1998, the stereo blared Willis Alan Ramsey's self-titled and only album, a classic from the 1970s Austin-Americana scene.

"No shit!" Miller said. "He just did a couple of songs with Lyle Lovett on that *Step Inside This House* record. Do you know that one?"

I fumbled through my center console to find the double-disk Lovett case. "Right here."

"Well then," Miller said, rifling through the jewel cases. "What else you got?"

By the time we reached the boat ramp on the Big Hole River, he had played songs from half a dozen albums, and we were, as they say, old friends. The bankside cottonwoods had yet to yellow, but the edges of the leaves were hinting fall, as was the sky—low dark clouds creeping lower—and the river carried a pewter cast that added expectation to every riffle, every run. With Miller standing in the bow and his good friend JH seated in the stern, I rowed upstream of Browne's Bridge to fish an eddy river right that often held big, fond-of-tiny-mayflies trout. From the surface of the eddy, a dozen such trout sipped *Tricos*, black-bodied, white-winged, mosquito-size mayflies that hatch near dawn, molt in the first hour of light, mate in the air soon after, then spin and fall spent, imagoes, by the fishing hour. On a still, low-ceilinged day, the angler might find a veritable carpet of these tiny creatures caught in the surface film of the water, the steely snouts of persnickety fish nosing through a figurative duckweed of bugs.

With a small Parachute Adams, not a perfectly realistic hatch-matcher but an impressionistic one, Miller made the first cast of the day—how I can recall such a detail when I can't even remember to pay my power bill each month I don't know, but I swear on my fly box it's accurate—and the long thin lantern jaw of a brown trout slid out to the left of the pod to inhale the fly. Miller waited—hard to do on the first cast of the day—until the big brown turned down with its mouth closed before raising his rod tartly to set the hook.

First cast, the day made.

Later it rained so cold and hard that JH's gas station poncho proved worth a few cents less than the ninety-nine he had paid for it, and his soaked blue hooded cotton sweatshirt and T-shirt chilled him to the bone. We stopped for lunch under Silver Bridge and built a fire in the dry wash with wood that June's runoff had tossed against the pilings. JH stripped down to his jeans and stood rubbing his bare arms near the noisy flames.

"I guess I need a new rain jacket," he said.

Miller: "I don't see why."

Even though I was a rookie guide, the fact that JH likely had earned millions of dollars and managed hundreds of millions in investments but owned the cheapest raincoat a man could buy was not lost on me.

"You do need a new raincoat." I laughed, though I knew I should have carried an extra. Tom Harman had told me early on, when I returned from my first day of guiding to complain about a client who had inadvertently dropped my spare rod-and-reel combo, a Winston rod with an Abel reel worth half as much as my boat, into the river: "If you're pissed, be pissed at yourself. It's your fault."

When you're guiding, he went on to say, everything's your fault, from pickup to drop-off. Guy slips on the rocks and breaks his arm: your fault. Husband and wife get into a shouting match and end up divorced: yep. Someone gets hammered, falls overboard: indeed.

"Short of a heart attack," Tom said. "And even then you should keep some aspirin, some whiskey, and some decent reefer in the first aid kit."

WHILE TRAINING THE SECOND AND THIRD GENERATION of Bahamian bonefish guides during the rise of Deep Water Cay, David Pinder employed an equally rigorous, if more figurative, philosophy, one that asked his charges to focus inward and outward with equal intensity:

"I would always tell the young men: 'Look at your hand. Now look at your little finger. If you have a cut on your little finger, you might think your little finger hurts. But actually, your hand hurts. And if your hand hurts, your body hurts. Nothing is separate.' Let's say a guide knows where to find fish on every flat, but he doesn't know how to tell an Australian cedar from a native pine, or what a kingfisher's call sounds like, or how to be courteous—then he has a cut on his finger."

In addition to teaching tides, boat position, flats, and fly selection, David taught his lineage of postulants that the guide must pursue, as instinctively as any fish, a satisfied feeling inside the client, an elusive and lucrative quarry. This is the guide's philosophical foundation.

The guide's literal accomplishments depend largely on the depth of his practical foundation: memory. Memory of every success, and, more importantly, every failure, assures a better hunt the next day. I'll allow that I have no proof and that memory, as Keats said, should not be called knowledge, but I recall, with exactitude, what fly Miller was using on his first cast of that September day nearly two decades ago on the Big Hole. Most fishing guides, many of whom are repressed savants, would not balk at this assertion because (1) the choice of a Parachute Adams in such a fishing situation makes practical sense and possesses verisimilitude, and (2) their savant-like minds catalogue similar precise memories. When a guide amazes a longtime client by recounting with precision decades-old fishing experiences, the client often responds with, "How do you remember that kind of stuff?" The guide's stock response: "I get paid to remember that kind of stuff."

But that's *why* the guide remembers, not *how*. The how has something to do with the shot of adrenaline that courses through the bloodstream of the guide's body and fortifies such moments; when a huge brown trout winnows slowly out from an undercut bank to inhale the sport's grasshopper imitation, or when a previously vacant page of white sand becomes suddenly punctuated by the singular wake-push of a cruising bonefish, energy heightens, and the guide's mind is stamped for all time.

These instances, sharpened blades that cut through the brain's gray matter, propel one straight into a state of wonder, and the scar the blade leaves is the memory itself. Wordsworth called these "spots in time," and Native tribes of the Northwest called them "river teeth," likening them to dense, pitch-filled knots of old conifers that a river's current could not easily erode. When the Buddha said that days spent fishing did not count against one's allotted days, he wasn't looking for a laugh. The moment when the downstream flux of the water and the downstream progression of a fly and the sometimes-downstream, sometimes-upstream, sometimes-sidelong swirl of a trout's take—the moment when all this aforementioned movement is met by the time-stilling stun of the hook set—stands outside time.

Incongruences

And so, being unable to find peace within myself,
I made use of the external surroundings to calm my
spirit, and being unable to find delight in my heart,
I borrowed a landscape to please it.
Therefore, strange were my travels.

—T'U LUNG

Although they each traffic in lines, most poets, anglers, and farmers are natural enemies of organized society. All three groups share aspirations of solitude, self-sufficiency, and enlightenment; but unlike poets, anglers and farmers can scarcely appreciate the weather without calculating its effect on their piscatorial or agricultural aspirations. Just landed in Freeport after a few months away, I sat in the taxiing airplane taking the stout north wind quite personally, watching the Bahamian flag stand tight as an ironed shirt against the sky.

Extending from a black triangle, the stripes on the flag— aquamarine, gold, aquamarine—stand for sky, sand, and sea. With modest hopes of evolving from tourist to traveler, I had trucked a few books onto the plane, and even my tertiary in-flight exploration into the islands' history made clear that had the earliest Bahamian inhabitants flown a banner, a wide bolt of red would have sufficed, signifying bloodshed. My skimming also confirmed my suspicion that, since Columbus, most white visitors to the islands had stayed just long enough to exploit resources or people—and, like any self-respecting poet, I was wary of cliché.

In casual conversation today's Bahamians are often mistakenly referred to as "native," but the first Bahamians of whom there is any evidence were the Ciboney, a tribe displaced, killed, or absorbed around AD 500 by the Lucayans, a Taino-speaking people who originated in South America and colonized the Caribbean in huge dugout canoes. Powered by seventy-some rowers per hundred-foot boat, the Lucayans used their vessels to hop from island to island. And with pace: they had to outrun the cannibalistic Caribs, whose chief concern was enslaving Lucayan women and castrating their men, who were first larded up on pig and coconut to ensure tender flesh for eventual consumption.

Eventually the Lucayans pushed through the islands we now know as Jamaica and Cuba, and settled in Exuma around AD 600, but like sharks on a distress scent, the Caribs were not far behind. By the time Columbus, who according to Ralph Waldo Emerson never discovered an "isle or key so lonely as himself," came across the Lucayans on San Salvador, he noted scars on their bodies, and through sign language was told of ominous tribes on neighboring islands. A bit more humane than their oppressors', the Lucayans' diet was comprised of fish and plants and the hutia, a small rodent, as well as the meat of conchs, whose shells they used to temper palmetto-ware pottery.

Despite the violence they had endured, the Lucayans were a peaceful people, gracious to Columbus and his men, who originally assumed that the tribe practiced no religion and would thus be quick converts. In fact the Lucayans had a highly evolved faith that revolved around a male and female godhead as well as belief in the afterlife. Ceremonially they snorted a potent narcotic powder derived from a perennial tree's seed-pods called yopo, which caused psychoactive visions. One such vision experienced by a chief foretold the undoing of his society at the hands of "strange blond men in winged canoes."

Columbus himself had red hair. But the arrival of his fleet of winged canoes in San Salvador in 1492 coincided with the destruction of the Lucayans' culture nonetheless. After returning

to King Ferdinand of Spain with captives, Columbus was ordered
to raid "the useless islands" of the Bahamas and over roughly five
hundred journeys the Spanish enslaved nearly forty thousand
natives. Originally these captives fetched four gold pesos each at
slave markets, but this price skyrocketed to 150 pesos per head
when rich pearl beds were discovered off the coast of Trinidad
and the Lucayans' aptitude as divers was revealed.

Preying upon the Lucayans' belief in a peaceful afterlife to
the south, the Spaniards corralled the natives onto pearl-diving
boats with promises of paradise. By most accounts all Lucayans
who didn't die at sea either committed suicide or died of Europe's
great hospitality gift: smallpox. All but vanquished by the early
1520s, Lucayans left traces of their culture in the language of the
New World: *avocado, barbecue, canoe, Carib, cannibal, hammock,
hurricane.*

From the early fifteen hundreds to the mid–sixteen hundreds, the Bahamian archipelago was largely devoid of human
occupation until a small group of English colonists—Puri-
tans and their freed slaves expelled from Bermuda for failing
to swear religious allegiance to the Crown—settled on Eleuthera. Living on fish and subsistence crops, these "Eleutheran
Adventurers" had the islands to themselves and early pirates
until 1670, when six Lord Proprietors of South Carolina were
granted the Bahamian islands by King Charles II. It was under
their rule that Charlestown, later to be named Nassau, was
erected on New Providence Island. For the next half century,
pirates as distinguished as Blackbeard and Anne Bonny made
harbor and frequent ambush in the islands but dispersed when,
in 1718, the Bahamas became an official Crown colony and the
Brits clamped down on piracy.

By the early 1780s—after the islands had fallen briefly to the
Spanish and been recaptured by British American loyalist freeboo-
ter Andrew Deveraux—roughly fifty thousand enslaved Africans

originating from central Africa and the Bight of Biafra had pop-
ulated the region. In 1783, recently evacuated from New York
in avoidance of the Revolutionary War, the first "loyalist blacks"
(excluding Deveraux's slaves) arrived in Abaco—some four hundred American-born blacks, many listed as "free" or "formerly the
property of _____." The colony's population increased by some
seven thousand when American loyalist refugees and their slaves—
many of whom had been promised freedom for taking Britain's side
in the war—arrived from Florida and South Carolina.

By 1785 slaves were a majority of the colony's population,
had formed the labor backbone of an unsteady cotton trade,
and were, according to one historian, "at least as varied in class,
culture, motivation and their ultimate fate as their fellow White
émigrés." At one point the colony's population included African slaves, transplanted American slaves, British colonialists,
American loyalists, and free blacks, the latter of whom often
supervised plantations. In 1787 the former governor of Virginia
(the same politician who had promised American slaves freedom for displaying loyalty to the Crown in the Revolutionary
War) became governor of the colony and immediately called a
tribunal to investigate certain blacks' claims to freedom.

On Abaco this inquiry led to armed conflict; two years later,
perhaps in response to the Abaconian conflict or the Haitian
uprising led by Vincent Ogé, the Bahamian assembly decreed
that "all the Negroes, Mullatos, Mustees, and Indians should
register with the Secretary their names, ages, address, family,
sex and color, under forfeit of their freedom." After registering,
these "freed" people were forced to perform menial labor, with
threats of fines or physical punishment for those who refused.

By the time emancipation arrived in 1834, a cotton-planta-
tion economy was well established on several islands, but due to
relatively poor soil (because of the same limestone that serves
as an ideal underlay for saltwater flats) and insect infestations,

the burgeoning trade remained undependable. Some historians assert that following emancipation, the colony's labor methodology became even more exploitative because of a labor and truck system that highly favored the white mercantile elite. In the growing colonial capital Nassau, for instance, merchants even imported Aegean spongers to establish a racial hierarchy. Freedmen became subsistence fishermen, sharecroppers, and peasant laborers where whites held deeded land, or attempted to establish squatter's rights on out-islands and unclaimed parcels. Many blacks manumitted from Royal Navy–seized slave ships found that freedom meant only deeper levels of poverty. Gradually the population in the islands grew with the settlement of these freed Africans, but colonial proslavery ties were not completely cut, with Nassau serving as a major supply base for the American Confederacy as late as 1865.

The capital's economy benefited greatly from US Prohibition as well. Shortly after the United States passed the Eighteenth Amendment in 1919—at which point the colony's population was two-thirds Afro-Bahamian—the Bahamian colonial government opened the trade of alcohol on Prince George Wharf, and for the next fifteen years spirits trafficking produced great revenue on the island. Prohibition's end, however, throttled the Bahamian economy. And while the next decade saw Nassau sprout into a budding tourist destination, much of the Bahamas floundered fiscally.

Two hundred miles to the north, the west end of Grand Bahama was little more than pine forest and swamp when Virginian Wallace Groves arrived in the early 1940s. Just released from a two-year prison term in Connecticut for mail fraud and the sale of fake securities, Groves soon negotiated the purchase of 114,000 acres (at less than three dollars per acre) and began to assemble an empire of casinos, resorts, and port infrastructure. Through the legal and political manipulations of Bahamian minister of finance Sir Stafford Sands, Groves, himself holding a doctorate of law from Georgetown, eventually came to hold over two hundred square miles of Grand Bahama, a mass of land just eighty miles from Florida that was exempt from Bahamian immigration law and much taxation, and governed by the Grand Bahama Port Authority, over which Groves presided. The Bahamian government made such tax concessions in exchange for the port authority's developing commercial and free-trade interests on the island, and Groves did not fail to hold up his end of the bargain. By 1965—just two years after Sands received a million-dollar legal retainer from the GBPA—416 companies operated under the authority, many of which were criticized for luring a criminal element to the island, and, according to a 1967 *Life* magazine expose, linked to Meyer Lansky's mob syndicate. In 1968 the undisputed founder of Freeport sold his interest in the port authority for $80 million; in 1978, five years after the Bahamas became a free and sovereign country, he sold the affiliated Intercontinental Diversified Corporation for nearly forty million.

A LITTLE OVER THREE DECADES LATER, I AM RIDING EAST again from the city Groves founded in Freddi Laing Jr.'s shuttle van, past Freetown, Gambier Point, High Rock: villages made up of bars, convenience stores, and churches. If the Bahamas were a coin, these backwoods hamlets would be tails, the hardscrabble, character-illustrating side, opposite the more polished, patriarchal heads, port towns such as Nassau or Freeport where the steel-drum music of Junkanoos blares on the wharf each evening as tourists leave cruise ships with fresh tan lines and plastic bags filled with duty-free rum.

I am anxious to reconnect with David at his home in McLean's Town, the conch-cracking capital of the world, one of the last small settlements in a chain of small settlements. To our left stand the pineyards, a dense forest of Australian pine and thatch palm from which seeps a heavy, dank wood smoke, the result of a fire caused, Freddi explains, by either a rogue lightning strike or the cops hunting for a stash of marijuana. We round the bend near North Riding Point Lodge, a well-known bonefish destination, and head into the last straightaway, the road ahead vacant save for the birds and moths and dragonflies spraying away from the van. It's the end of September, the trough of tourist season, and Freddi is hurting for business.

"Man, it's my birthday, and I don't have any plans."

"Really? Why not?"

"I don't have any plans, man, 'cause I don't have any money."

I haven't seen Freddi in months, but what I had thought of as our rapport seems to have endured. Perhaps his skills as a conversationalist go hand in hand with his ancillary role, but I take strange comfort in the fact that he has reengaged me with the tenor of our old conversations. To be remembered, however faintly, while driving east down the archipelago, gives me the sensation of having slipped time, or of having reentered a landscape in which time, illusion though it may be, progresses less gravely.

When he isn't preaching at the Pelican Point Church, Freddi captains the shuttle van from Freeport to Deep Water Cay. The lodge charges $300 per round trip, and takes a modest cut, so when the lodge is busy—January through May—Freddi is flush, carting two, sometimes three groups of guests per day from the Freeport airport to the McLean's Town docks. But the shoulder seasons can be a bit slim, he says, "And on top of that, there's no basketball to watch!"

A hard-core NBA fan, Freddi opines with the fervor of a sports–talk show host hopped up on Red Bull, but the National

Basketball Association players' association and the teams' owners are locked in a labor dispute: "Millionaires fighting millionaires for more millions," Freddi says.

"Still," he says, "I'm picking Miami and Oklahoma City to go to the Finals. If they have a Finals this year." Whether wheeling the Odyssey or standing underneath the cross at church, Freddi commands his pulpit.

When I ask how he evolved into a preacher-slash-driver, he says, "Blood will tell. My father, Freddi Senior, is a preacher, too. We passed his church about ten minutes ago, in Pelican Point. Remember that guy out in front cutting the grass, I honked at him? He's been driving for Deep Water Cay since Mr. Drake first bought the island in 1957, since before I was born. We have to drive to support our habit."

I'm quiet for a moment, assuming the worst: booze, coke, some newfangled concoction that the kids have cooked up.

I take the bait: "What habit is that?"

"Preaching!"

I'm tempted to jest that I've guided fishing trips for over a decade to support my habit of poetry writing, and that one high-minded bard once referred to the poet as the "priest of the invisible," but I've watched the mere mention of "my craft or sullen art" deaden too many conversations over the years to risk the aside.

Freddi explains that, while the Spaniards established their share of missions and the English later peppered the Bahamian archipelago with Anglican churches, most Christian Bahamians currently practice with intense pride what one might call a Baptist-Pentecostal hybrid. On some out-islands, a type of folk magic derived from West African origins, called Obeah, is practiced, but "the unofficial Bahamian national church has a lot of singing, a lot of preaching. And a *lot* of *a-men*-ing."

Freddi's cell phone rings—some R & B rendition of a gospel tune; I hear the male lead backed by the female troupe croon,

"Jesus, you are my rock!"—and he fumbles for the vibrating device on the console. He's driven this road so many times that I don't envision the van center-pinning a pine, despite the statistics on distracted driving. Freddi is talking but suddenly I can understand only every tenth word: *club, yeah, Freeport, Deep Water Cay, Pinder.* Bahamians often speak to other Bahamians with this unfathomable speed and ratatouille of dialects; we tourists must simply wait for the translation.

After Freddi hangs up, I ask leadingly, like some tactless graduate student in postcolonialism, if this self-actualized evolution of Christianity in the Bahamas represents a departure from types of worship that white rule established?

Freddi responds graciously: "You know, man, I don't really know. I do know that if you really want to dot the i's and cross the t's, we're not even the first Bahamians." Freddi pauses and looks out the window at the passing pines, as if he were scanning the swaying trees for listeners, as if he had said something he shouldn't have said.

"There's a lot of the history of the Bahamas that, I admit, I don't know much about, but I do know that when I was growing up, late seventies, early eighties, I didn't even know what racism was.

"My daddy's generation, though, now that's a different story. You remember back there a little ways we passed the New Star Club? It's owned by Romeo Bridgewater now but years ago, back in the sixties, a white man owned it. Back then my father was driving Mr. Drake and some friends to Deep Water Cay, and Mr. Drake says, 'I'm hungry, Freddi, let's stop and get a sandwich.'

"They stop and go inside, all five of them, and sit down to order. Well the owner comes right up to Mr. Drake, points at my father, and says, 'This man will not be served in my establishment.' Mr. Drake gets in a huff and stands up to leave but my father insists on waiting in the car."

"What happened?"

Freddi shakes his head. Outside the van a mockingbird scales invisible tiers of sky, and disappears into the pineyards. "Mr. Drake brought him a ham sandwich from inside. But that's a kind of racism I never really saw in the Bahamas."

Far better with moments than I am with dates, I place Freddi's anecdote on my less than thorough Bahamian Time Line somewhere in the decade before Miller's first arrival. As the van nears the end of the two-lane, I look out the window with a grateful nod for Miller—an envoy who always travels with hopes of receiving rather than taking—and the trust he's established here, which has opened doors for me. I recall our last ferry ride together, on which he confided that he read *Moby-Dick* every year, as a touchstone of sorts, to gauge his own growth and understanding. He was somber, hewn with the recent news of his father's passing back in Saint Louis. I asked if there were any other annual rituals in which he partook.

He looked out across the infinitely attributed water, and back at the island: "Coming here each year."

A FAIR NUMBER OF SENIORS AND JUNIORS APPEAR IN THIS story—a naming convention that reminds me unfavorably of the few days I've spent at country clubs—but alas, I didn't name them. Like Gil Drake Sr., Jefferson Miller Sr. had married into a fair amount of wealth before he first brought his son to Deep Water Cay. Senators, international corporations, a large parcel or two of land: his wife's family had it all, and yet his Ford's Missouri license plate read "WGAS."

Who Gives A Shit.

For nearly three decades this cantankerous enigma hosted groups of high-test Saint Louis anglers, many of whom were accustomed to being served back home by black "help"; nonetheless he loudly insisted they spend at least one dinner across the channel at Alma's, to which he always invited the guides and their families—and after which he stealthily picked up the tab.

In the Second World War, the Old Timer, as Miller Sr. came to be called at Deep Water Cay, had served extensively in the South Pacific, and upon returning to his base in California he'd proceeded directly to a barber for a haircut. He was exceedingly tan after many months at sea, and the barber, mistaking him for a person of color, turned him away without a word, pointing to a sign on the door that read, "No coloreds any kind." Rather than explain his ethnicity or show off his navy stripes, he told the racist holding the scissors to "suck eggs," and kicked the door shut on his way out.

On the boat, club guides coveted his presence because he could cast twice as far as most guests could, told the crassest jokes on the island, and when the fishing got slow sang songs that began, "In the shade of the old apple tree / That's where she showed it to me . . ." Invariably he favored Walter Reckley as his guide; "Fishy Wally," he called the rotund, unflappably smiling former mentee of David. And the affection was mutual.

For someone whose most available tender is words, I find myself too frequently at a loss for them. I excuse myself by claiming that a poet is taught to rely on silences, to value what is not said, but that late April afternoon on the grave ferry ride, I was quite simply failing to express sympathies to Miller, and frankly relieved to see Walter Reckley amble across the aisle and put a jocular elbow to Miller's ribs.

"Tell me, Miller," Walter said over the loud twin Mercury outboards, sitting down next to his favorite client's son. "How is the Old Timer this year?"

"Well, Walter," Miller said, clearing his throat, "I'm very sorry to tell you, but the Old Timer didn't make it through the spring."

Walter tilted his very round head over his soiled shirt collar, as if he were scanning for a book on a low shelf, and pulled his grin into a fist of skin.

"He passed very recently, my friend," Miller said, explaining that the news was quite fresh, but that given his hard-core nature the Old Timer wouldn't have wanted anyone, especially his son, to mope around funereally if he could have been fishing instead.

"He's gone, the Old Timer? I can't believe it, man," Walter said, proceeding to launch into a fugue of fond memories, jokes, the entire shade tree song, until, before he could catch himself, he was weeping into his khaki guide-shirt sleeve. Rubbing tears into his elbow, he looked south toward the open water. Outside of a Márquez novel, I wanted to ask my old professor, when does a whore cry over a john?

When he'd composed himself, Walter said:

"Remember how he always fished those dark-brown flies? Even over a white sand flat. He'd say, 'Walter, what fly do you think I should put on?' And I would say, 'Something real light colored, Miller. Something pale.' And he would say, 'OK,' then tie on that goddamned dark-brown thing! Sometimes he drove me bat-shit crazy."

Miller sat there nodding, his own eyes brimful. It could have been the boat's tilting on the waves, but it seemed that for a moment the two men leaned toward each other, perhaps to embrace, then shied away, each afraid to embarrass the other. So they just sat there smiling, looking into each other's faces. And by now everyone on the boat—Americans and Bahamians, fathers and sons, anglers and guides, the boatman Kenny, the dockmaster Audley, even those of us who had never met the Old Timer—was a little wet in the eye.

Who was it said we were invented by water as a means of its getting from one place to another?

Arc of Acuity

> LEAR: Yet you see how this world goes.
> GLOUCESTER: I see it feelingly.
> —WILLIAM SHAKESPEARE, *KING LEAR*

Near dusk Freddi pulls the Odyssey into McLean's Town. As the van slows, two brown dogs with coiled tails emerge from the wayside to greet us, nipping at the vehicle's rolling tires until Freddi parks at the quay. Above the water, underneath an aluminum awning, a man is filleting a fresh snapper in the last of the September day's light, running the blade in one firm swipe from just behind the fish's caudal fin to the hinge in the tail, laying back the struts, holding the meat briefly to the shrinking sun to inspect it before setting it aside. Beyond the docks a heron stands up to its bony knees in the low tide, a few seabirds fly by squawking.

After unloading my luggage, Freddi reaches out his hand. "Have a good time with David Senior, man. I will catch you on the flip side. Maybe the boys will be playing basketball by then."

"On the flip side," I say, slipping some cash into my right palm and shaking firmly. "And happy birthday."

Freddi looks down and smiles without opening his hand.

I walk up the marl road wheeling my suitcase over the ruts. For the moment I am overdressed in my sport coat and slacks, encumbered by my backpack and shouldered fly rod case, self-conscious as I pass two T-shirted McLean's Town men playing dominoes on a front porch. I nod at them, feel what James Agee called the swerving of small-town eyes, and acknowledge my slight alienation. Momentarily this alienation morphs into a trepidation at seeing David again—the man I have come to understand, in the time since our last meeting, as the taproot of Bahamian bonefishing, a revered man whom even one tonally reserved how-to 1980s outdoor writer called "a Bahamian of unperturbable dignity," a man whose life, what I know of it from research and conversation, seems to verge on the rare heroic. My mind flits between what others have told me about him, what I've gleaned, what I've imagined, and I fear the actual might crumble what my mind has made of him.

Then the evening cools instantly—the freshening, day's exhalation—and the reddened sky bruises. A waxing crescent moon brightens, comes in crisp, and I am instantly happy to have my coat. I hear a deep jovial voice coming toward me out of the near dark:

"Hello there. Good to see you, sir."

It's David walking down the road toward me with a slight hitch in his stride, his blue house barely visible behind him; he must have seen Freddi's van coming down the road, and come to meet me. As he nears, his wide smile comes into focus, then the white writing on his black hat that reads, "God is good all the time."

"New moon," he says. "Big tides."

"You're limping," I say, shaking his hand, which is nicked up from repairing outboard motors, I assume, from hand-lining snappers from the wrecks. His spindly fingers envelop mine. He grips tight, placing his index finger on my inner wrist, on my radial vein: a bond.

"Yessir. Pinched nerve. I need to do a therapy."

Though David stands six feet tall, I remembered someone six foot five, such is his legend, his inner stature. A picture of rectitude, he is nevertheless built like a deceptively dangerous welterweight, as if he could throttle you if he absolutely needed to. A hint of red highlights the otherwise dark-brown skin of forearms that still appear capable of poling sports around the East End for a living. He wears a plaid collared shirt, tucked into khakis rolled up at the cuffs. His feet—flat, elephant-wrinkled, half as wide as they are long—appear to have spent more days exposed to the elements than they have spent shod.

From David's neighbor's yard, a rottweiler emits a throaty growl that says, *I'm too lazy to get up off the grass and harass you but don't think I couldn't chomp your calf if I felt like it.*

"Nasty?"

"He's nice," says the man whose surname name means "keeper of stray dogs." "But he's always pulling down stuff, knocking trash cans over."

A small scooter driven by a heavy, hunched man zips past us, then quickly doubles back, its driver hollering, "Hey, Speedy, gonna see you down at Leroy's tonight?"

"No, sir," David answers. "Going down to Alma's. Fried-conch night."

Without further word, and with an almost comic lack of acceleration, scooter and driver double back again, and the engine's tinny ruckus disappears into the dark. We walk along the wayside past skiffs with names like *Kirchie's Ghost*, *There She Goes*, and *Lady Grace*.

"'Speedy'?" I ask, as we turn up David's driveway.

"It was my boat's name back in the day. Most boats are named after women. The sailors, they'd be gone a long time." He stops at the door to his house and turns to regard the black water. "You know the old song, 'How I love my love.' But I was always the fastest with the motor and so they named my boat *Speedy*."

David's kitchen is dimly lit and two of his grandchildren sit at a round table over dinner plates smeared with peanut butter, beside a Bible and a bulbless lamp.

"Jason," David says, and I reach out my hand toward the hesitant boy. "Stand up and shake his hand, son. And this is Trinity."

I offer my hand to the young girl, too, but she pops up and hugs me suddenly around the waist, then steps back and chirps, "My momma says I can hug the white man who's coming to visit cause inside we're just the same."

With a clothes iron in hand, Trinity's mother Delcina appears presently from the living room and laughs deeply. Rake-thin but stout as an anchor line, she embraces me lightly with her free arm, her smile the spring from which her daughter's openheartedness doubtless wells. As Freddi says, blood will tell.

She holds up two button-down shirts. "Daddy, you'd better come tell me which shirt you want ironed."

"Yes, ma'am. The brown one, please."

A little while later I'll hear Edwin, David's son, call from the living room, "Pa, come see this! The Lakers might trade Kobe Bryant," and think: Speedy, Pinder, Daddy, Pa, Senior: everybody calls David something different.

And he calls everybody sir or ma'am.

If Jesus was right, and the eye is the lamp of the body, then Senior's lamps were all but snuffed out by the mid-1990s. Half a century of searching for grayish-white fish in wind-broken, sun-refracted grayish-white water without the aid of polarized glasses had taken its toll on his eyesight. Although he could see well enough to get the boat away from the docks and onto the flats, and though he knew the tides as well as the mangroves themselves knew them, and though he knew, better than anyone in the world, when and on which East End flats the bonefish fed, and though, to this late day, he insists otherwise, Senior struggled in his late years to see the actual fish under the water, and his vision often doubled.

But some men don't need sound eyes to find fish.

Miller contends that despite his failing sight, the affable

Senior knew the movements of the local fish and nearby flats so thoroughly that many of the club's anglers requested his services regardless. Reid Sanders, managing partner of the Deep Water Cay Club from 1988 through 2001, once apologetically referenced Senior's failing eyesight to a longtime guest, and the guest responded with a huff: "David Senior hears bonefish—he doesn't have to see them."

Cracking conch early one evening, Senior contests the notion altogether.

"I never had a hard time seeing the bonefish. They say that's why they wanted me to retire but, no sir," he says, whacking a pronged shell with an old cutlass. Earlier in the day I watched him harvest these conchs from the windy channel. Numerous times he had to wedge the pole against his hip to slow the skiff from drifting too quickly over the tide-bent turtle grass. Then he'd draw his pole from the water, cock it, and stab the dry hooked end into the water. He looked like a ninja sparring with an invisible foe. Then he'd raise a football-size, slime-covered conch shell from the water, spin the stick again, and clunk a dripping conch into a white ten-gallon bucket while the skiff skated away on the wind. I'd placed his display among the highest ranks of works, and one that required ample visual acuity.

"Maybe there was a time," I say, nudging, hinting at something Reid Sanders had told me by phone, "that you couldn't see the fish as well as the other guides? Like, you could see them at one hundred feet, but not six hundred?"

"I never had any trouble seeing any fish."

To the south a storm threatens but the wind is indecisive: carrying one minute a hint of warmth from the west, the next a brisk threat from the north. Senior reaches his hand down into the weathered white bucket for another conch, but the bucket is empty.

"One year, late in my career, I think it was this same time

of year, there was a guest who came down and said, 'I don't want to go with that old guide.' I had fished him before. He was one of those guests who thought he knew the flats better than the guides, even though he had only visited a handful of times. 'Well, David,' he'd say, 'what do you think about that East End'—even though he didn't know the tides—'what do you think about the cemetery?'

"The manager put the wife in my boat instead. Man, I fished her hard, all morning, all afternoon, but a front had the fish off-kilter. Sometime after lunch she said, 'Do you think it's time we gave up?' 'No ma'am.' I told her, 'The only time I think it's time to give up is when this boat hits the dock.'

"No matter how quiet a guide gets, he always wants to catch fish more, far more, than his client does. Well, right at East End Creek, I spot a tailing fish, swing the boat so that the wind is at her back, and tell her to cast *on its nose*. The line was a little long, but the wind brought it back, and fifteen minutes later we were putting a twelve-pounder—biggest of the season—on the board at the lodge.

"Her husband came back after a slow day, and the first thing he sees at the dock is this big, double-digit bonefish. He says, 'Well, someone had a fine day! Who caught this whale?'

"The manager walked right over and whispered, 'Your wife did. She was fishing with 'that old guide.'"

This catch occurred near the end of Senior's career—I imagine the bonefish, mounted on a large gaff against the white plywood brag-board painted with the club's old logo, long removed from its element, desiccating in the sun and wind—and wonder if the club could have simply paid to make sure Senior received the medical attention he needed, and retained him to train new guides. Then Manager Sanders asserts the club "got [Senior] some doctor's appointments in the States but he refused to wear the glasses. In the end we threw him a big retirement party."

Ultimately management—one of more than a dozen teams under which Senior worked—elected to cut a severance check instead. In 1995, as a reward for his nearly forty years of service, they offered $18,000. That's roughly $450 a year, or $37 per month, or $8 per week. Or an extra dollar and a quarter for each of the fourteen thousand days he worked for the club. For the man who, with a machete, cleared the mangroves from the island for the lodge to be built, cleared ground for the runway so private planes could land, and then led visitors to the fish and new ways to hook them.

Senior stares down at the fresh conch squirming on the cleaning table. The conch with its single inky eye stares up at its Maker.

"I was disappointed because I still felt, after all those years, that I had a lot to learn about the flats. As long as you live, I used to tell the guides, you can find something out about the fish, something new. Bones are just like people: sometimes they wake up in the morning and they just ain't ready to be social yet. In the early days I was on the face of every magazine in the world. So maybe I quit while I was ahead. But they didn't really offer me much choice."

Like a boat coasting over the shallowest of shoals, Senior left easy, though he felt as if he'd "been hammered."

"I had never been anything but happy in life until I began to think back on the time I'd given Deep Water Cay. I went through every single day in my mind, from when Mr. Drake first hired me through my last guide trip, and I couldn't think of a day when I hadn't done what I thought was best for the club, the island.

"All the money's gone. Long gone. Down to the nickel. Some went to the children. We took a cruise, Cozumel, St. Thomas, St. Lucia. I would love to get to Panama but I don't know where the money's coming from. I tell Delcina I want an iPod. She laughs. 'What's an old man like you want an iPod for?' I haven't got any money, but I sure enjoyed those forty-one years. I don't look to them for my reward, though, I look for my right reward. When a man works with a just heart—"

Senior's voice trails away as he looks to the south. It is just before dark, and the lodestar hangs bright above a crown of reddened cumulus.

"Sometimes I get so lonely that I ain't out there with those guys."

HORIZON'S SO PERSISTENT—YOU TAKE ONE STEP TOWARD it, and it takes one step back. Precisely where does the water stop and the sky begin? I reference this unchartable point because the lines between biography, story, and myth seem even less definable, more arbitrary.

And yet I've asked Senior's son Jeffrey down to East End from Freeport for the afternoon to help me redress the issue of Senior's declining vision. With a decidedly quiet Delcina, we sit town-side on the high dock overlooking the channel and the lodge. The tide is dead low and the flat looks more like a desert crossroads than a fertile habitat for game fish. On the air hangs the rich ripe scent of exposed and drying turtle grass.

"I worried about him after he retired," Jeffrey says, "when he was having all those headaches." Jeffrey allows that after the club nudged Senior not so subtly into retirement, his father's vision did indeed begin to decline, but asserts that it wasn't Senior's eyes' fault.

"I tend to mark time by the storms, so this would have been just after Hurricane Fran, I think it was called." Regarding big tropical storms and hurricanes in the Bahamas, it's not a question of when but how hard the weather will hit, and, if the storm is big enough, what its name will be. Poststorm, the destruction always resembles the last poststorm destruction: uprooted palms tossed onto the porches of disheveled cottages, grounded boats, unidentifiable human accouterments strewn from the palms, a generally anonymous chaos.

After Fran, Delcina interjects, Senior got a headache so severe "that it closed both of his eyes." The left half of his body possessed no feeling, and when he left his bed, he stumbled from room to room, grasping at chairs for balance. One night that August, she had a dream. "I saw Daddy lying on the bed," she says. "I saw a skull, and an X-ray, and on the X-ray there was a small round white thing inside the skull. I saw Daddy's heart beating, but very slow."

A week later doctors in Freeport found the massive cyst, slowly growing and, they worried, cancerous. Fearing they couldn't safely remove it, the Freeport medical staff suggested that it simply might be Senior's time to pass.

"Daddy called some of us to his bedside," Delcina recalls. "He said, 'I'm safe.' So we thought he was leaving us. We started holding vigil. But he said, 'All the people around look worried. Don't worry. If I live, I'm gonna live for the Lord and if I die I'm gonna die for him. And if he don't heal me, I know he could.'"

A few days later Jeffrey, back on the flats guiding, was hurting something fierce.

"My client, Bill Bell, he's a brain surgeon. He saw my pain and asked me what's the matter, so I told him about Pa's decline, and he just turned to me and said he would be happy to do the surgery. I told him I certainly appreciate the gesture but we can't afford it.

"He said to me, 'Jeffrey, what do you always tell me when I blow a shot on a bonefish?'

"'I say it's not a problem, Bill Bell. We'll find another one.'

"'Well then,' he said, 'it's not a problem. I'll do the surgery for free. You and David Junior can take me on a few complimentary guide trips someday.'"

Originally the Bahamian doctors thought Senior's tumor was the size of a golf ball, but in Winston-Salem Dr. William Bell unearthed something the size of a salad plate, a glove. Like a conch, but hard as a knot of wood. They went in under Senior's upper gums and cut straight up. Had to scrape it out with a razor. Half of Senior's face was numb for six months. Technicians biopsied it, and aged it at sixty-seven years old. Senior had been living with the tumor since he was a boy, since he first walked the white sand foraging for snails near Pelican Point.

"There was this school of fish," Senior says. He has risen from his afternoon nap and, walking slowly across the dry burrows of hermit crabs, tracks of killdeer, gulls, he seems a bit reserved, as if he's privy to the fact that I was talking about him while he slept. Wind through the living palms' fronds makes the sound of a child make-believing she's a ghost. Some weathered Styrofoam washed in from who knows where runs up on shore, and backpedals in the out-current; runs up, backpedals. The dusty evening light labors through a forest fire's haze that tinges the air with an eye-tearing odor.

"There was this school of fish," Senior repeats, "about two hundred, maybe three. I watched them one afternoon. The sighting was so good you could see the pink on their noses from where they'd been digging around in the bottom. And it was the strangest thing: this one fish, he was swimming with his white belly to the sky, on his back. I thought maybe he was injured but he would right himself and swim like the rest of them for a while. Then he'd go upside down again. I don't know what he was doing. Eating stuff the school had kicked to the surface? Maybe just clowning?"

Now the rum-colored light is so acute and angled that Senior looks almost caricatured, his features etched, his eyes pellucid. What keeps troubling me, what won't seem to stay shut away, is the matter of his sight, whether it was ever bad as the club managers asserted, or whether it stayed true. So like some two-bit lawyer rephrasing the same question over and over to a witness on the stand, I ask:

"You never had trouble seeing the fish?"

"No, I never did."

I resign myself to the notion that we're leaning toward the apocryphal here, because by all accounts, from the maids to the guests, Senior endured a lengthy period of time during which life, and particularly the elusive fish at the core of that life, was at best a blur.

Senior points out at the water and the breaking waves, makes a swishing motion with his hand as if to mimic that lone fish's inexplicable movements. He shakes my hand and grasps my shoulder, then turns toward home and supper.

Walking toward the docks in the waning day, I'm startled by a birdcall, and turn to watch a mockingbird harry a hummingbird from a trumpet-shaped *Allamanda* flower, the smaller bird's wing-beats audible as it floats off like a knuckleball. A warm wind runs up the coast and over me, sewing-thread thin, a tiny trace of the element stopping me in my tracks. I stand precisely where the water meets the sand, wondering if, given time, the patient scooping of the surf might empty me of myself. Then I watch the sun extinguish itself without a trace of residue, and make a stride into the bay, a long way from the latitudes of home.

LIMITS OF

PURSUIT

Minds Like Fish

It might be natural for us to have minds like fish
in a dwindling stream.

—DŌGEN

A good friend of mine hunts or fishes 350 days a year. Montana, Wyoming, Idaho, Nevada, Utah, Arizona, Oregon, the Florida Keys, Yucatán, Belize, Alaska, Chile, Argentina. Trout, salmon, steelhead, bonefish, tarpon, permit, snook, grouse, pheasant, partridge, seven species of quail, Himalayan snow cock, deer, elk, moose. Using "fair-chase" methods, he has caught, shot, and eaten an unfathomably diverse range of species of which Audubon himself, who also killed them to study them, would have been envious. I live convinced that he is one of the world's essential outdoorsmen. That kabbalistic notion that there are a few dozen holy people on the planet keeping the earthly sphere from spinning into the chaos: this friend of mine may well be one of them. He talks to himself while he fishes. Without a shred of self-consciousness he speaks to his quarry: "Come up and grab that fly, you scaly dawg." When he handles a trout before releasing it, he speaks to it again: "That spot on your cheek's red as Mars!" He fishes so often that his dreams are filled with fish and while sleeping he continues his conversations: "You gonna stay hunkered in those weeds or come join us in the land of the living?"

They hear him.

You've never heard of him, and if he has his way you never will. What energy the world devotes to fanfare, he devotes to hiddenness. When he's not drifting in a boat, he wades the river no matter how swift the current, so as not to leave footprints on shore. He converses with birds and four-legged mammals far more often than with human beings. He regards each cast as a dharma gate. Once at dusk after fishing for steelhead in the rain forest of British Columbia, he found himself surrounded by a pack of growling wolves: the finest moment of my life, he says. A fabulous memory of earth. When he ties a triple surgeon's knot, lashing a length of fresh tippet to the end of his leader, he ritually scans the circumference of his surroundings, owl-like, all 365 degrees, and in gratitude acknowledges the place. He wets the line with his tongue, and pulls it taut, knowing what he's tied to.

Think of a cloistered Emily Dickinson stitching her poems into elaborate caches. Though even Miss Emily intimated that her work would last.

THERE IS SUCH LITTLE VIABLE FAME IN THE FLY-FISHING world that those who actively seek it out via self-promotion—television shows and endorsements—appear buffoonish, and those upon whom genuine well-earned respect is authentically bestowed are often resented by a large portion of the contingency. The guiding world is a little like, say, the world of academic poetry, in that the proverbial pie has shrunk to the extent that those looking for a piece of it act cagey at best, catty at worst. The phrase *famous poet*, like *famous fishing guide*, constitutes a whopping oxymoron. So when compliments are dispersed, it is often with reservation and qualification: "He's a great fisherman, but he shadowed so-and-so for years, then stole his fly patterns and pimped out his water." "She's a wonderfully obscure poet, a perfect combination of Swift's irreverence and Berryman's desperation." Prime examples of why, like writing, fishing is a perfect job for those who prefer talking to themselves to talking to others.

Gil Drake Jr. grew up awash in an equally ephemeral sort of fame—one in which Deep Water Cay Club guests and employees knew exactly whose child he was—and was thus, as the owner's son, treated with some degree of reverence or resentment, and became, for better or worse, insouciant about this status.

"We ran eight guides back then," he tells me by phone from his home in Homosassa, Florida, "and I was the white one. I got away with it legally. But it's a good law nowadays," he says of the Bahamas' rule against non-Bahamian guides. "It's right."

Maybe he never possessed a nostalgic vein, or maybe the salt, sun, and time have leached any shred of sentiment from his heart, but he recalls his time at Deep Water Cay as if it were a birthmark.

"When my father first bought the island in 1956, he wasn't looking for anything but a place to go fishing. Did he think it would become the most famous bonefishing destination in the world? Nothing of the sort."

When asked to speak about Senior's guiding abilities, about whether or not Senior helped advance the saltwater fly cast, Drake's voice reveals a hint of impatience, as if he's answered too many David Pinder questions over the years.

"David Senior was a fine guide, but he never used a fly rod."

Never used one, or never used one well?

"David Senior never used a fly rod."

After coming of age and moving on from Deep Water Cay, Gil Drake Jr. moved to the Florida Keys and by the early nineties (not long before I arrived there for a short deadhead stint with a fake ID and a fly rod, and failed to catch bonefish while camped on the flats at Bahia Honda State Park) had caught more big tarpon than anyone from Key Largo to the Marquesas. Having established a kind of cult status in the guide bars of Islamorada, Big Pine, and Duval Street, Drake Junior moved up the coast to Homosassa, where he spends his days guiding anglers into migratory tarpon that often approach two hundred pounds, their mouths wide as ten-gallon buckets, their scales twice the size of a silver dollar. Though he doesn't advertise, his booking calendar fills by sheer word of mouth. He is legend, if you will, a cave-dwelling guru sought out by only the most serious aspirants.

Many who have been around the sport long enough to call themselves aficionados think of Gil Drake Jr. as one of the most knowledgeable bonefishermen in the world, meaning he knows, in the words of one such aficionado, "more than the famous guys." Meaning he knows more about a sporting niche the general reader has never heard of than a bunch of middle-aged white guys the general reader has never heard of, either. Meaning he hasn't published how-to books or hosted television shows, or sold his fly patterns to Orvis or L.L.Bean. Meaning, sure, there've been a few articles written about him over the years, and he's spoken of reverently in guiding circles, but he's probably too busy fishing, learning more about his craft each day—his learning curve still rising but only imperceptibly at this point—to invest significant time in self-promotion.

Maybe he thinks it indecent. Maybe, growing up the son of a man who owned an actual island in the Bahamas, he felt no need to climb some proverbial career ladder, illusions that such ladders are. Or maybe he intuited somewhere along the line that detachment focalizes, and that the pure blue flame of attentiveness extinguishes anything paltry that might approach.

A DAY SPENT FISHING—TO RECONSTITUTE ONE AUTHOR'S take on the act of reading—is arguably a wasted day. But a *lifetime* spent fishing—a lifetime spent inevitably more attentive to the earth and its wild creatures than to one's own ego, a lifetime

spent pursuing not only the seen but the unseen and intuited—
now that's an entirely different matter.

Senior, who on days off from guiding would often pole an
empty skiff just to see how close he could get the bow to a school
of bonefish, likes Kobe Bryant's Los Angeles Lakers these days.
He takes a cup of tea and an egg for breakfast. Some days he
doesn't mind a bowl of oatmeal, too, which he usually fixes for
himself while Nicey, his wife of sixty-two years, sleeps, often
spent from tending to the grandchildren late into the night.
Two decades ago, when Senior was still working at the lodge
and keeping one bonefish per day for the table, Nicey would
prepare the fish for the family, broiling it with lemon and salt
and pepper on the skin, a little paprika. Senior liked a few flakes
of cold bonefish in the morning. He would pull the remains
from the icebox and pick through the ribs for a bite that put
the day's quarry on his mind, before taking the ferry across the
channel to guide.

This breezy morning the man who was once famous to the
fish stands outside barefoot and surveys the front yard. Stripped
to its axles, a rusty silver Chevy Astro van looks as capable of
transporting passengers as does the nearby beached johnboat
with a splintered hull named *Steady On*. Atop a sawhorse
two Evinrude motors hang, their mechanical guts splayed out
beneath them. Above the blue house—it's been this deep blue
for at least four decades, for as long as anyone can remember—
between native pines and Australian cedars, above two satellite
dishes and a half dozen plastic barrels filled with casting nets, a
warbler darts back and forth, singing the same song it sang six
months ago in Montana: *witchity-witchity-which-which*.

As for ambition, that strange form of anger, the bird has
predictably little to say.

Too tired for much mischief, a yard dog lies in the pine tree's
goading shadow, an empty aluminum can near his nose licked

clean and glinting like some bit of treasure washed ashore. The can catches Senior's eye and he bends gingerly to pick it up, takes aim at a burn barrel: about fifteen feet, a free throw. Clouds crowd in for a better look. He leans away smiling and tosses a high arcing hook shot that rattles into the trash. The pines dispense their applause.

On Vision

To be an artist was to see what others could not.
—PATTI SMITH

It's a crisp evening in McLean's Town, the night sky flecked with hordes of stars, but Mervin Thomas, grand-nephew of Senior and current dean of guides at Deep Water Cay, says it's going to rain tomorrow.

"Merv," I protest, "there's not a cloud in the sky."

Having worked out a deal with the lodge, I'm back in East End hosting a group of clients who fish with me each year in Montana and hoping a storm doesn't ruin our opening salvo. Seven paying guests meant a complimentary trip for me; but aside from the freebie, playing excitable client for a week serves to remind me how amped up my own guests are when they fish the West, a tiny translation that promises to revivify my work on the river back home.

"Yeah, man," Merv says. "I realize that, but my hip hurts."

After battling chronic pain for a decade, pain caused by leveraging with a push-pole the weight of his client-laden boat against his hip, Mervin had the right joint replaced eighteen years ago, halfway through his guiding tenure, and instead of fading in his second act built a reputation as one of the fishiest guides in the world, a dignified man whom the legendary angling television star Flip Pallot has called, along with Senior's grandson Meko, one of the two best flats guides he's seen anywhere on the planet.

Merv wears his postguiding uniform: khakis, red mesh jersey, Miami Dolphins cap, and sunglasses. He's ridden his spiffy cruiser bike down to Alma's because he doesn't have a car, only drives once every other week, borrowing his brother's sedan to head up to Freeport, to make a deposit at the bank. The young teller usually gives him a wink and a "Thanks, Mr. Thomas," when he hands her the rubber-banded roll of cash, but the larger teller showcasing a large gold cross at the north end of her ample cleavage promenades around the bank for a while pretending she has something else to do before handing him a receipt with palpable disdain. A look that says, *I'm not sure how you make your money but I certainly don't approve.*

This is Merv's routine. The other guides buy homes, boats, SUVs they soup up with high-end audio systems; they get married, drive into Freeport every Friday night, take cruises, but Merv dons his red jersey, he rides his nice bike to Alma's to see if someone in the kitchen will give him whatever's left over in the fry basket. A couple of hush puppies, a fritter or two. No matter how late it is, he doesn't remove his sunglasses. Why waste your eyesight on humans when you're saving it for fish?

"If my hip hurts at night," Mervin says, surveying the goods that Alma has just brought out from her kitchen—heaps of crab salad served in Styrofoam cups, conch fritters drizzled in a feisty sauce, and fried conch slabs I plan to hand-to-mouth like potato chips, "it's gonna rain in the morning."

"I wouldn't bet against Mervin," says David Pinder Jr., Senior's eldest, who is down from Freeport to dine with his father for the evening.

When Senior was a boy, carrying sharkskin to peddle to the boot makers and shark livers to sell to the man who made oils, it took him three days to walk from McLean's Town to West End. Now his son drives an hour down the highway to pay his father a visit. In the midnineties, after guiding for Deep Water Cay for nearly twenty years, David Junior migrated along with his brother Jeffrey to Freeport to traffic the north shore waters. It's windier up there, with fewer islets and less lee, but the bonefish are bigger, averaging six or seven pounds to the East End's three or four.

"The seeing is far different down there, too," Senior explains, declining the platter of conch fritters I offer. "For the more resilient angler. You could go down there and look for weeks before you knew what you were looking for."

Nonetheless, the Pinder brothers have made a fine living in Freeport, which sports a bit more nightlife than McLean's Town. David Junior would never say it, but McLean's Town, where churches outnumber bars, is a bit too prudish for him. He's gracious in his father's presence, but one senses that part of him that remains the boy who left Bumpkinville for the big city, or more realistically a port town that at least hosts grocery and department stores, and remains vibrant due to a steady influx of optimistic tourists and opportunistic locals keeping straw markets and cigar shops. And where he can write his own story.

In an age where an athlete can become "epic" for one slam dunk or touchdown catch, it's hard to use the word *legendary* in earnest, but David Pinder Jr.—plank-shouldered, tall and thin, appearing from atop his skiff's platform like an extension of his push-pole—is indeed legendary among Bahamians. Thought of by many as one of the best saltwater fly casters in the world, he routinely impresses guests by casting an entire hundred-foot fly line *without a rod*, generating line-speed with his arms and hands alone. Consider that, to accomplish this, his arm movements must replicate the pliability, strength, and fulcrum of a nine-foot, eight-weight graphite rod. Once, at the International Fly Tackle Dealer Show in Denver, David Junior helped a particular rod company sell its whole stock of saltwater gear in ten minutes, after guests witnessed him casting at the rod company's booth. "David didn't even particularly like the rod," said a friend of mine who witnessed the feat. "But it was like watching Mario Andretti drive a Volkswagen—suddenly everyone wants a Jetta."

Was this casting grace inherited? I've watched Senior approach a fly rod with the air of a former knight who, because of an unspoken code of honor, refuses to pick up an old sword. And yet when the prime minister visited Deep Water Cay to honor the club's legacy, it was Senior who was asked to commemorate the event by casting on the dock, and Senior who garnered the applause. Meko, the most elegant caster I've ever witnessed, still brags on his grandfather's ability to time and power a shot.

So to Gil Drake Jr.'s assertion that Senior never touched a fly rod, that final stop in a symphony of knowledge that swirls around the bone, I ask: How does someone who has never touched a fly rod end up with a lineage like this? He is father of eleven children, grandfather of forty-eight; Senior's family is not a tree so much as a grove. The same can be said of his guiding family: of the fifteen most gifted guides in East End, ten were trained by Senior, and the rest trained by guides he trained. Senior's fame may have faded, but what does recognition matter to a man who has endowed generations of his offspring, and an entire community, with blood-level intimacy with an ecosystem and its prized fish?

Regarding fishing lessons, David Junior is quick to credit his father, but more than a bit reluctant to fall into rank in other matters. For a long time he headed a band the brothers Pinder formed called the Gospel Vibrations, comprised of David Junior on the drums, Jeffrey on keyboard, and William on bass. They cut several self-produced albums, one of which is playing loudly from the single, suitcase-size, borrowed-from-the-church speaker that is Alma's sound system.

Senior, who used to play the guitar, or *gidda* as he calls it, claims he taught the boys as much about music as he taught them about guiding, but there is some scoffing on this matter.

"Pa, come on, now!" David Junior says, looking to Mervin for some help.

Senior: "I can still teach them how to knock out a melody."
David Junior yells toward the kitchen: "Alma, what did you
put in this dip? Pa is saying crazy things!"

At this Merv stands gingerly from the table, adjusts his
sunglasses, and clears his throat.

"Boys, I thank you, but I'm in for the night. Gotta dig out
my slicker for the morning."

My trust in Merv's fishing know-how is such that if he told
me to cast into a parking lot puddle, I would start lining up the
shot, but the acute stars above leave me laughing off his mete-
orology.

At dawn, though, I will wake to a sky chock-full of clouds,
step outside, and feel Mervin's prophecy fulfilled: a warm drop
of rain on my nose.

MY LONGTIME CLIENT AND FRIEND PETER AND I DRAW
Mervin for our guide, and he stows our rods and motors away
from the docks without much of a greeting. We're pushing
north with the rest of the fleet, six boats, and Merv points at the
quickly bruising horizon, looks at us, shakes his head. Another
guide's skiff edges up to ours and its driver glances north, then
shrugs at Merv, as if to ask, "North?" Merv nods a not-quite-af-
firmative nod, then eases off the throttle to let the other skiff
slide past. Seconds later Merv calls an apparent audible, whips
a 180, and slips the Hell's Bay skiff into a small creek mouth.

"Those guys think they're gonna outrun that front. I've been
watching the satellite weather all morning, though. It's coming
a lot quicker than they think."

Within an hour, Merv's split-second decision proves to have
been a deft one, as between us Peter and I land eight bonefish,
most of which were tailing alongside the mangroves on the
north bank of the fifty-yard-wide creek or suspended between

the banks, offering texture to the otherwise slate-blank screen of water.

Now that he has a few fish in the bag, Merv has loosened up a bit. He's humming a little tune from the skiff's platform, happy, I wager, with his decision to stay in the backcountry. I sense he's too humble, or too superstitious, for I-told-you-sos, but I want to know what he was thinking when he tweaked his game plan.

"Merv, did you have this spot saved in your back pocket for a day like this?"

"You're a guide. You know. You have a kind of catalog of memories in your head, right? I haven't come in here for three or four years, but when I woke up today and I saw it was a front moving real slow from the north, I thought to myself, 'You know, the fish up in So-and-So Creek usually seem happy on a heavy weather day.'"

"Is that what you call this place, 'So-and-So Creek'?"

"Either that or 'Such-and-Such.'"

By now the birds are singing the way they do right before a deluge.

"Get up on the bow, Peter"—Merv points his pole at one o'clock and I see the referent, a tailing bonefish about fifty yards away—"we've got time for one more before the storm gets us."

Peter and I have been going fish-for-fish all morning, and his eyes widen at the chance to best me by one. He steps onto the bow, strips line, readies the coils, and composes himself with the remove of a pool shark, lit cigarette hanging from his lips, about to sink an eight ball in a crowded bar. He starts his back-cast, but Merv reins him in: "Give me a second, man. That's a happy fish. Not going anywhere." Gradually easing the skiff closer, clocking the bow around to give Peter a better angle, Merv whispers, "Not yet, not yet. OK."

Peter laces out a cast that lies down soft as a shadow, and

strips the small crab imitation once, briskly, before the pale fish tips down and the line comes tight. A few minutes later he holds the fish, and asks me to take a picture of its tail, which we had seen sashaying above the water several times while Merv positioned the boat.

"You talked me into this one," Peter says to Mervin, slipping the pale five-pounder—a typical but nonetheless priceless Bahamian bone—back into the brackish water. "Highly efficacious. I would have blown it without you in my ear."

"Most people," Merv says, "would have tried to make that long cast, but I'd seen his tail a dozen times from the platform so I knew he wasn't going anywhere. Most people like to make a big long cast that shoots out and lands real heavy."

He pauses long enough for the audience to register that by "most people" he means his present anglers. Then the punch line—"But most people forget they're trying to catch a bone-fish"—just before the rain begins to fall heavy on our Gore-Tex roofs.

By afternoon the front has lifted, there's a sunstruck line of five barracuda staking out the flat at Goggle Eye Bank, like a group of bullies waiting for the skinny kid to walk into the locker room for his beating. The skinny kid is a fatigued bonefish Peter is about to land and release. I can sense Mervin eyeing the group of blade-shaped predators, keeping the boat between them and the bone. It's not that Peter has played his fish exceedingly long, either—the fish just seems to have burned its reserves on its first and only run into the backing. We stand guard as the freed fish scoots off and buries its nose in the turtle grass, then slip down the flat in search of another target. Momentarily we're startled by what sounds like a roar of water, and Merv spins the skiff around: three 'cudas at two hundred yards, trailing the winded bonefish. I know how this will end—the fish will pin the bone like well-trained English setters running a pheasant through tall-grass prairie—but can't peel my eyes from the pursuit. When the smallest of the three 'cudas finally nabs the four-pound bonefish, it chomps sloppily on its prey, nose to tail.

"That 'cuda's eating my bonefish like it's a Twinkie!" Peter says.

"Merv, how many bonefish do you think a barracuda like that eats per year?" I ask, amazed at how quickly I'm able to fall into the role of "Sport": tangling my line, forgetting gear at the dock, requesting something from the cooler just after the guide has started to motor the boat, asking unanswerable questions like the aforementioned.

"I don't know, Chris," Merv says, "but I tell you what: I'm going to make some calculations while you jump out of the boat and catch up to that school there." Mervin aims his push-pole over my shoulder to where the bright-green turtle grass tapers into sand the color of an almond's center. "Mostly small fish, but I think I see a real big one at the back of the group. No time for your waders, man. Just go in your feet."

If there is a greater pleasure in angling than stalking bonefish barefoot across an urchin-less sand flat, I have not encountered it. The sand is pocked from where the school was rooting, but other than that the soft floor is unblemished. I hear Merv's whistle from over my shoulder and turn to see him pointing intently toward the school, which looks to be comprised of fish the size of hoagie buns, their noses, red from rooting, the color of budding raspberries. I decide not to cast at the schoolies, and noticing my nonchalance Mervin whistles again, this time holding his hands apart, wide as his shoulders. I laugh as the school banks away from me. Then I see what Mervin has been pointing at: bringing up the rear of the group, a bonefish he would later call the one of the biggest he has ever seen, dead or alive, and estimate near fifteen pounds, grubbing off what the smaller fish rooted up. I throw a lottery chance of a cast into the rattled assembly, which spooks with enough energy to shake a house.

Back in the skiff, chagrined, I apologize to Mervin for blowing the shot.

"You told me you thought you saw a big one in the group, but I didn't—I don't know what I was thinking."

Merv smiles, ever gracious.

To paraphrase Francis of Assisi: the saints kept silent when they wanted to talk.

Though Mervin's no monastic. When I first fished with him as the guest of Miller, I didn't feel my modest cash gratuity was sufficient, so upon returning to the States I loaded up an old MP3 player with thirteen albums by AC/DC, his favorite band, and sent it in care of the lodge. The next spring when we shook hands at the ferry dock, Mervin had his earphones on, as did I. I smiled and gave a thumbs-up. He smiled and gave a thumbs-up, then took an earphone off:

"What you listening to?"

"The Faces," I said. I knew what he was listening to.

"Rod Stewart's old band. I like them, man. What song?"

The answer seemed too perfect, but it was blaring in my left ear nonetheless: "'Just Another Honky,'" I said, and Merv fell out laughing.

"That's a good one, man. That's not bad at all."

Miller has fished flats across the globe for thirty years, and insists that he has learned more from Mervin about the art of bonefishing than from any other guide. He calls Mervin one of the best teaching guides he has ever encountered.

Why is this? I ask.

"Because he says the least."

IT WOULD DOUBTLESSLY EMBARRASS HIM TO KNOW THIS, but I call Mervin "the Magician" for the way he seems to make fish appear on a previously vacant flat. Often I have found myself wading a flat that he has chosen, scanning for fish, but drifting listlessly into one of those piercingly quiet moments during which the reverent can stare briefly into his own soul, or toward the possibility of a soul—before the white sand between the turtle grass suddenly gains texture with moving shadows and tails.

Usually if Mervin catches me in one of these dehydration-induced poetic trances, he will simply whistle and point in the direction of the fish, but occasionally he'll ad-lib.

"Chris. Group coming in over your left shoulder. They're going to split us."

"I don't see 'em, Merv."

In which case, to get his point across, Merv can become a measured realist:

"Your eleven o'clock. Point your rod. Good. Right there."

"I still don't see 'em."

Or an exuberant impressionist: "Keep looking just under the surface. They're that minirevolution that's about to run you over."

Sometimes I get the feeling that the fish are always there, that it's just my attention to them that waxes and wanes. As Henry David Thoreau said: "Music is perpetual, and only hearing is intermittent."

WE'RE WAITING OUT THE LIGHT JUST EAST OF RED SHANK Cay, named for the seldom-seen roseate spoonbills that used to frequent this outer mangrove-choked islet. I'm on the deck hoping to make Mervin—who has run the boat a long way in search of a big fish—proud. Earlier this season one of Mervin's clients won a prestigious Redbone fly-fishing tournament with a thirty-two-inch ten-pounder from this same flat. I try not to think of that fish as the cloud bank retreats and the light, that gem-cutter, reveals the flat's infinite facets.

"Going away from us," Merv says. "About two casts away. Big boys. I'm gonna see if I can pole back around and cut them off before they get to the bank."

Though his grunts are muffled by the wind, and though the pole slides silently in and out of the water, I can tell Mervin is straining to get me in position. I think about his bad hip, about how, spooked by a bad experience with some postsurgery pain pills, he refuses to take even ibuprofen to relieve the pain. *Do his hard work justice*, I tell myself, which is another way of saying, *Don't poleax these boys on the head.*

"OK, I'm gonna swing you and put them at ninety feet. That's the best I can do. OK, give me a—ah, shoot! There go the lights."

I look back over my shoulder at the clouds and estimate the duration of the shroud at five minutes. These fish will be long gone by the time the light breaks through. Long gone. I give some thought to my last botched cast, the headwind I overcompensated for, think about how, at dinner last night, someone referenced the sea cucumber's ability to increase virility—in this manner the radiant vacancies between fish are passed.

After good minute of silence, I say, "We can head in, Merv. It's been a great day."

"But this is not a game you play quittin', my friend. I believe," he says, stretching that second *E* sound out as far as he can, "I see a tiny mud. I'm gonna ask you in just a second here to give me a shot at twelve o'clock"—Mervin's trust-eliciting tone is like that of a parent coaxing a child to jump off a diving board into a pool. "OK, stretch one out. A little longer. Lay it down."

I still don't see the fish, but I don't see the wake of a spooked fish, either.

"That's good. Short strip. Strip again. OK, he's on it. Let it sit. Long strip. You got him."

And so I do: an eight-pounder suddenly fleeing the flat, the stirred sand rising in its wake like dust behind an outlaw's horse. Listening to the line shearing through the water's surface, I stare disbelievingly at the small mud by which Mervin located the fish. "Tiny" was a vast understatement; it's about the size of a salad plate. Just a little puff of smoke, the kind a magician produces.

I find myself wishing for the instantaneous faculty to see these fish the way Mervin does, but Dogen's centuries-old staff smacks against my head: "Your belief in spontaneous enlightenment is heretical!"

The Tug

It's a wicked life but what the hell
Everybody's got to eat.

—BOB DYLAN

In the nearby Florida Keys, just a hundred miles to the north-west, what fisheries biologist and University of Massachusetts professor Andy Danylchuk, with whom I've corresponded frequently, calls "regional economic contributions of the recreational industry centered on bonefishing" generate a billion dollars in revenue per year. A decade ago in the Bahamas, the sixth-richest country in the Americas, whose ten-cent piece features an image of two bonefish, direct expenditures on guided trips brought in an estimated $20.6 million. In 2013 the Ministry of Tourism declared the bonefish a $141 million annual crop. In a country where tourism, per Danylchuk, "accounts for more than half of the gross domestic product, making tourism the largest single contributor to the country's economy," bonefish might as well be coins, fresh from the mint.

Only a decade after gaining its independence from the British Crown in 1973, the Bahamas found itself at a crossroads. Government officials, including Prime Minister Lynden Pindling, faced widespread allegations of drug trafficking after an NBC report, "The Bahamas: A Nation for Sale," aired. Journalists claimed that Pindling and other officials had accepted bribes from Medellín Cartel cofounder Carlos Ledher, who had boasted to Columbian media that the cartel had established control over Norman's Cay in Exuma, the central base for smuggling cocaine into the United States. Public discontent led to a commission of inquiry, which found that Pindling—

knighted by Queen Elizabeth in 1983—had spent eight times his reported total earnings from 1977 to 1984, and had received over $57 million in cash.

Even a sleepy, end-of-the-road town like the one at East End saw its share of smugglers. These days, down at the dock in the evening, the boats arrive with the setting sun and the men slap large snappers and grouper onto the filleting table, carry buckets of snapper, conch, and lobster. A few decades ago, the same men might have been whispering under their breath about the whereabouts of a cocaine drop near Sweetings, or a flivver that had dropped out of the sky and was still smoking on an unnamed cay. A local named Cauley told me that though the drug-running days are all but done, just about everyone in the region with a boat made a few dollars helping a suspicious craft navigate a channel or a spit.

"In the eighties a guy offered me ten grand just to get him through the Tongue," a channel known for its dangerous hydraulic pulses. "I took it, yeah. But just that once.

"Some nutty times back then. I remember a plane crash-landing on the club's airstrip and spilling four tons of pot out of the cargo bed. The crew and passengers died on impact, so a few of us locals divvied things up and started making trips to Freeport. My cousin Edroy, he was nuts when he first got that money. He sold his lump, paid cash for a brand-new truck, got ripped, then wrapped the new Ford around a palm tree on the way back to McLean's Town. You'd think he learned his lesson, but you know what he did? Hitched right back into Freeport, bought another truck with folding money and drove it home."

About the same time the Freeport Police Department figured out that Edroy had paid cash for two new trucks in less than twelve hours, the Bahamas Ministry of Tourism realized the bonefish, a renewable resource, had become a high-test commodity. For decades the fish had been regarded by most

Bahamians as kitsch, an undesirable rough fish with which select tourists liked to play, but now the value of the fish—a raw material that had existed undervalued for centuries, like a mineral perceived worthless until it becomes the essential ingredient in some pharmaceutical cocktail—had become glaringly apparent. Expeditiously, the government had to decide which it wanted on its hands, drug blood or fish slime. With haste it chose the latter.

TODAY, A QUARTER CENTURY LATER, THE $700-PER-DAY price of a guided fishing trip (gratuity *not* included) and the $20 million in recent Deep Water Cay improvements raise the question: How exactly did a fish become an industry?

To begin with, anglers spend up to 25 percent more than other tourists, and in communities such as McLean's Town where alternate sources of revenue don't exist, money generated by recreational bonefishing, Danylchuk writes, can float the proverbial boat. Tourism, it has long been reported, accounts for over 60 percent of jobs in the country; the staggering $150 million-a-year stat has inspired attempts to calculate the value of a single bonefish. Charlie Smith, founder of Andros's famed Bang Bang Club, has estimated that each live bonefish is worth a thousand dollars to the islands' economy.

Feasible? If we take an aggregate flats-fishing day at Deep Water Cay during which an angler catches four bonefish, and divide said fish into the cost of an average plane ticket, taxi fare, tab for two days' lodging, food, and guided fishing ($3000), we're looking at over $650 per caught fish: strong assurance that the thin gray film, the once-living skin of a bonefish that rubs off on our dying own upon release, is a fairly pricey slime.

And yet, despite the Bahamian government's effort to guard its unofficial minister of tourism against mass harvest, studies show that populations of bonefish have decreased steadily over the past few decades. Commercial fishermen continue to string monofilament gillnets across the mouths of tidal spawning creeks each year, a practice that stunts population growth, as well as unintentionally collecting sharks, barracuda, turtles, and dolphins. For generations bonefish have supplemented the earnings of subsistence fisheries, the bony, tedious-to-prepare (and, with its seventy-eight vertebrae, tedious-to-consume) fish tending to be sold to individuals or small restaurants in rural communities. Due to the availability of commercially produced food items and the social stigma of bonefish as a poor man's food, there has been a downturn in its harvest, but the damage may already have been done: research suggests that the bonefish population today is at best in troubled waters—one study puts the declination rate at roughly 20 percent over the past thirty-five years, a rate directly correlated to the rate of mangrove declination—and at worst—based on decrease rates of up to 90 percent since the late 1940s—only a ghost of its former self.

"IN THE EARLY DAYS," SENIOR SAYS, "THOSE FISH WOULD come looking for you."

It's Sabbath at the Pinder house, and wafting through the open front door the scent of sizzling conch is too much for the yard dogs to resist—they prance into the kitchen, teats drooping to the dirt-covered linoleum.

"Yessir. I have seen more fish in one school than most of these guides today will see in a lifetime." As he describes the school of bones he once saw spanning the entire channel between McLean's Town and Deep Water Cay, the square half mile dark with fish and their shadows, I find myself wishing his tale were merely a yarn.

"Rasta, Blackie!" Senior yells at the dogs, their noses tilted up to the stove.

In her white nightgown at the stove, Senior's daughter Linda points a spatula at the dogs. "Get! Get out of here."

As the dogs shuffle out, in shuffle Linda's children dressed in pressed white button-downs and black sweater vests, ready for the service their uncle Edwin will preach in an hour. Linda flips the pale-yellow pieces of conch in the skillet and begins to list Senior's children:

"There's Cynthia and Edwin, Ludell and David Junior. William. Della's next, she lives on Marsh Harbour. Then Grace and Joseph, and Delcina. Me. And Jeffrey. Half of them, almost half of them, guides."

Linda, a champion conch cracker herself, even tried to convince Deep Water Cay to hire her as its first female guide—"I've been going in the boat with my father for thirty years," she says, "I know where all the fish are"—but the club balked at her proposition, saying they needed her skills in the kitchen.

"Apparently," I offer, "they'd never heard of Dame Juliana Berners."

Linda looks askance as she parries the conch to three plates, which she carries to the table balanced against her hip. "Come, boys. Sit down to eat. Edwin. Daddy, come have a bite."

Edwin slips into the kitchen past a lingering Senior, pats the boys on their heads, and sits down on a stool. With his eyes closed and head bowed, he appears to be waiting for Senior to bless the food, but after a moment he looks up at me and shrugs:

"This is a fishing family through and through. The kids these days, though, they swap good spots with their buddies while washing the boats. They don't care. When I was young, we used to say, 'I got fish, I got fruit, I got a good woman. What more do I need?' These boys, most of them are more concerned with getting a day off so they can get into Freeport and spend some money in the city. Tune up their sound system. Buy the new Jay-Z T-shirt. Some of them never even heard of Pa."

. . .

ACROSS THE CHANNEL, OVER AT DEEP WATER CAY,
the guides are readying the boats, stashing thermoses and coolers beneath the padded seats of the lodge's $40,000 Hell's Bay
skiffs, checking gas gauges, stowing thousand-dollar fly-rod-and-
reel combos, relishing their last solitary moments of the day.
Inside the lodge's dining room guests polish off eggs Benedict,
chat drowsily about the degree to which their hangovers will aid
or impede their fishing, check the NASDAQ on their tablets, or
even answer e-mails, perhaps from someone back at a Cleveland
cubicle who nonchalantly queried, "How's it going down there?"
     On his iPad, a man taps out an answer: "It's rough, my
friend. Waking early and walking down to the beach at dawn
to look for tailing bonefish before breakfast; fishing all day; jog-
ging at dusk; stashing a rod in the mangroves and waiting for
the flood tide and more tails; all before a dinner of lobster soup
with curry and red pepper and chunks of crustacean, conch ceviche, and fresh grouper washed down with a peachy Sancerre.
Very rough."
     Some of the dozen guests here are well-known actors best
known for their cinematic portrayals of comic book charac-
ters, some have made their millions in the market, some have
inherited their fortunes from fathers who visited Deep Water
Cay five decades ago—back when Senior earned less than one
one-hundredth of what today's guides earn for trips. One fiscal
whiz at the table, wondering aloud what else in the world besides
a bonefish trip has appreciated so consistently, jots down some
figures on a napkin and calculates: $5.00 for a guided trip in
1958, adjusted for inflation, which has been about 3 percent per
year on average, is $26.80 today. If the average guide trip is now
$700, that means the annual increase in guide costs has been
about 10 percent per year, roughly three times the inflation rate.

LONG BEFORE THE CLUB OWNED HELL'S BAY SKIFFS
with their ten-foot-tall poling platforms, Senior ran a fifteen-
foot fiberglass Mitchell johnboat and stood atop the twenty-five-
horse Mercury to better survey the flats. In those days guides
cut and peeled their push-poles from pine trees, a practice that
lasted through the heavy Sea-Squid skiffs and the rudimentary
Dolphins, until the dynamo Hell's Bays, engineered with aero-
space technology to displace maximum water, arrived.

The only way to float an eighteen-foot-by-six-foot boat
loaded down with a quarter ton of people/motor/gas/tackle in
three to six inches of water is by displacement. For every eight
pounds of weight, a gallon of water must be displaced. Even an
aircraft carrier could float in six inches of water, given sufficient
surface area, given the right engineer. The flatter the hull of the
boat, the shallower it can run. But in waves or on long runs, less
forgiving flat-bottomed boats ride like a strut-less pickup on a
washboard road.

Like most advancements in flats fishing, skiff development
trickled down from the Florida Everglades and Keys. There
the first skiffs were actually standard boats that guides had
customized—a nose chopped here, an angle rounded there—
and that they poled backward to reduce hull slap and push,
water movements that fish feel in their lateral lines. The original Bimini Bonefisher was constructed with native wood and
gunwales lined in horse flesh, a loud boat that guides could
pole only so shallow. They wanted a boat that wouldn't "slurp,"
though, a craft they could pole in a drop of dew. Today companies like Hell's Bay work with material borrowed from Boe-
ing, such as Kevlar, carbon fibers, polymers, and closed-cell
foams, that combine to form a craft that is stronger, lighter,
and quieter than steel. In the end the guides got their wish,

but as newly designed boats arrived ready to navigate the shallowest of flats, fish pushed out of their preferred feeding grounds and began to move farther and farther inshore—the distance between hunter and hunted never quite overcome, as if both parties were magnets.

And while visually the fish never ceases to mesmerize—a hundred bonefish threading a maze of mangrove roots above their shadows will remind the viewer of his last encounter with hallucinogens—it is to this day the bonefish's vast unknown quality that captivates anglers.

Only recently have we learned a modicum about its migratory habits, where it lives between birth and adulthood. It ranks among the wildest of creatures, says Thomas McGuane, "If a sensory apparatus calculated to separate them continually from man's presence qualifies them as 'wild.'" Since luck itself is a rarity on the flats, an encounter with the fish requires physical attention and determination, true grace coming—to steal a phrase from Martin Luther King Jr.—not by favoritism but by fitness. At this stage in its sport fish evolution, the bone's elusiveness has even transcended the realm of myth to become a cliché of sorts.

But the man who is the veritable impetus of this multibillion-dollar Bahamian industry, the initial fishing guide at the initial fishing lodge, who has been with the fish since the days when its dyed scales were used to decorate earrings, seems to know them more intimately than most. "They're a friendly fish," Senior says. "I've seen them out there porpoising. They seem to enjoy themselves. You want the truth, though? It ain't even half the fish that was here back then."

Generations

Children are our crop, our fields, our earth. . . . They
are the only sources from which may be drawn a life . . .
more knowing than our own.

—JAMES SALTER

Sandpipers, those little nitpickers, comb the wet sand for their
invisible meals as a wave recedes, then glance up and rush shoreward as another breaker spreads across the littoral zone. We're
walking opposite the shorebirds, Senior and I, along the southern
shore of Deep Water Cay, waiting for Meko and William, Senior's
son, to pick us up in the skiff. Today marks the first time these
three generations of world-class guides will have fished on the same
bonefish boat together, and Senior seems giddy with anticipation,
striding without a limp as he shows me how he would pole this flat
were he still guiding, how he would keep to the upwind edge of the
flat before turning downwind and aiming for the small bucket-size
depressions hemming the edge of the weed bed.

He starts to explain how quiet you have to be, how bumping the hull with the push-pole is the equivalent of farting in
church.

"I knew a preacher once," he says, chuckling at his half-
shared memory. "But there's no teaching poling. I used to take
out a book and tell the young guides to push it around the table
with a pencil, a little game like that, but you either see the fish
and the quietest way to them or you don't. There's no shortcuts
that don't spook fish. It's a noble profession. The ones who were
going to learn were going to learn—like William or Meko—
you could say I saved them some time, but the good ones would
have gotten there either way."

I suggested this family-plus-me outing at Alma's one evening under the assumption that the men fished together often,
but when I learned such a merging was a lacuna I became insis-
tent. It's a lag week at the lodge, so William and Meko aren't
missing out on any work; nonetheless we share a laugh at the
dock over how difficult it is to convince a guide, proverbial car-
penter whose front door needs to be planed, to go fishing on
his day off. Though I brought a camera with vague hopes that
the excursion might be article-worthy someday, it's clear to me
that for his descendants this venture is about getting Senior out
on his old playing field. Uncle and nephew seem thoroughly
roused, especially Meko, who initially begged off, citing family
obligations, but showed up having jettisoned his to-do list. He
shrugs. "I can cut the grass in the evening."

Half an hour later we're not too far south of Big Mangrove
Cay when William cuts the motor and orders me up on the bow
of the skiff. I try to defer—"No sir, I'm just here to take notes"—
but Meko, climbing up onto the poling platform, insists.

"You're our guest today," Meko says, sliding the graphite
push-pole through the flat water that resembles a pale-green
gelatin covered with Saran Wrap, "and you're going to catch the
first fish. We've got a big October tide working in our favor this
morning, but it'll be too heavy this afternoon to do much with.
So let's make it happen."

A few years from this moment, I will be able to reciprocate
Meko's generosity when, on a generous shared client's dime,
Meko and his family visit Montana to fish—but for now, like
some city-league softball player taking batting practice in the
majors, I climb onto the clean deck and peel from the reel sixty
feet of fly line, then step back from the coils.

From his seat, Senior leans over the side of the skiff to scan
the seafloor, to read its text: "They haven't been feeding on this
bottom. Yet." Almost instantly, as if by some spell he's cast, a fish

comes into Senior's view. "Here's one coming at nine o'clock," he says without much exclamation.

"Whoa!" Meko exclaims. "Pa can still see 'em! I'm up here on the platform and he beat me to that one."

If I myself could see said fish, I might wager that Meko was just pumping Senior up, letting the old guy feel like he can still play.

"Those fellas," Senior says, speaking of the management at Deep Water Cay thirteen years ago, "claimed I can't see anymore. Watch this fish doesn't get behind you, Meko. He's gonna hug that bank and then turn if you let him. I like this spot, though. I caught some of these fish's distant relatives."

Finally, as its tail cuts the bright pane of water, I see the big isolated single contouring the bank, lone wolf totally content to break fast in solitude.

"We're not gonna have a whole lot of time here," Meko says. "There's a school behind us that's seen us. If they mingle with our target fish here, it's all over. When fish get spooky like that I want to keep them behind the boat."

Senior: "Otherwise they go straight down the strip telling everyone, 'Something bad's going on out there.'"

"About eighty feet," Meko says, "he's tailing. Over there at ten o'clock now. Wait till he tips down again and then put it right on his nose."

No longer the lucky contest winner getting to take batting practice with the stars but the rookie called up and penciled in to pinch-hit, I lean into the back-cast—here is where the cameras would flash if there were cameras, where the footage would fall into slow motion were this a film—pause on the balls of my bare feet as the fly line's loop unfolds behind me, then drive the cast forward. My body is a door swinging open on the hinge of my right big toe, right hip, right elbow, right rotator cuff; then slamming closed, as I finish with my right thumb pointed directly at the fish, and my left hand tugs, at the last possible moment, the line, forcing the fly to perform a late bright somersault.

The fly glints briefly in the midmorning light, winks at us in its way, before falling into the foot-deep water. What happens next, I tell myself, is up to the fish. I have hit the first pitch hard, I have driven the ball.

What happens next is that the bonefish—so defined in the midmorning light I can begin to count its hundreds of holographic scales—swims up to my mantis shrimp, spots the imitation's plastic goggle eyes staring out of the sand, takes them for actual shrimp eyes, tips down, and sucks the fly in without deliberation. With a left-hand strip—I love this moment best, when the entire connection between fly and tippet, tippet and leader, leader and line, is most tenuous, stretched to its utter limit—the hook penetrates.

"Where's the camera boat?" Meko says. "I was filming a show last week with Flip Pallot and we couldn't get anything like that on camera. First cast of the day!"

After one blistering run, the fish flags and corkscrews at the water's surface alongside the boat. I keep the rod well bent, keep my mouth shut: I'm too superstitious, too surprised at my good luck to celebrate yet or accept Meko's backslapping.

"Warm water," William says, standing up, "warm as it gets all year. Fish tire quick."

Then, without warning, Senior stands up, too, leans over the hull and grabs the fish behind the gills, inverts it so as to disorient it, pops the fly free from the corner of its jaw, and slips it—

"Wait, wait!" I say. "Let me get a quick picture of you three."

"Pa, when's the last time you held a bonefish?" William says.

"About thirteen years ago."

I snap the picture and Senior releases the first bonefish he's held in over a decade, a stout six-pounder. His long fingers have cradled "plenty of thousands" of bonefish—the living bars of silver whose discovery has helped feed his children, grandchildren, great-grandchildren, and now great-great-grandchildren—but this particular one, if his smile is any indication, makes him radiate with pride.

"Man, I can't tell you how good that makes me feel," Meko says. "I was feeling the pressure up there. I was thinking, 'Please, God, don't let me fail in front of my uncle and my granddad.'"

You *were feeling the pressure?* I think. Though perhaps acknowledging the pressure, not coasting, not resting on his lineage, is what makes Meko, a guide of superior charisma and acumen, one of the globe's most sought-after teachers.

In *A River Runs through It* Norman Maclean said that he never prayed for a fish because he feared that his shaky faith would only be further challenged by prayers unanswered. I ask Senior if he ever prayed for good fishing.

"No, because the Good Book says seek first the Kingdom, not seek first a fish."

The three men laugh: the sure trunk and stout branches of a family tree leaning back into the brassy sunlight. Though Senior's cell-level humility likely prevents him from acknowledging it, I wonder if he sometimes glimpses the inheritance he's left his descendants: the occupational made sacramental. Alongside its crisply drawn reflection, the boat lifts and falls on the waves as if the water itself were inhaling, then exhaling.

"Some people don't like to get old," Senior says, "but I think it's when you can enjoy life. You're with your kids and grandkids. They like you and you like them."

Flickering briefly, like a turning bird's wings suddenly grabbing light, a disturbance of water brightens the inmost portion of the flat: another single fish, its tail shining like a miniature two-fingered peace sign. "Should I jump out and wade for it?"

"No, no," Senior says. "That's a flat you won't get too far on. East side of Big Mangrove Cay: you'd be four feet deep in two steps."

What has changed in forty years? The short answer is: Far less than that which hasn't—such as the actual geography of these East End flats. This side of Big Mangrove Cay has been muddy since before Senior first pushed a pole against its bottom, crushed a staghorn coral with the blunt end of the pine shaft, grunted inaudibly, pushed on. Despite the steady technological advancements in gear, the general appreciation of costs, and pending Deep Water Cay Club expansion, though, Senior is refreshingly unsentimental about the good old days. What's changed most significantly in the sport, he asserts, is the skill level of anglers.

"Today it's so much higher. The guests, they know how to cast, how to play a fish. But the enjoyment is higher, too. It didn't take much to catch fish back then, it was too easy. You just cast your fly out there anywhere *near* the fish, make a strip, and they're there. I believe I caught more fish on a little Pink Puff than a live shrimp. It didn't matter. But these days bonefish don't believe in luck."

WILLIAM HAS BEEN NOTICEABLY PENSIVE THIS MORNING. Aiming the boat at full throttle toward a black dot on the heat-blurred horizon, he sees me looking back at him and gives me a smile that seems forced, a thumbs-up. Later in the evening I will learn from Meko that William's Pinder's Ferry—the thirty-five-foot twin-engine boat with which he earns the bulk of his income—was T-boned by a cell-phone-distracted local boater while docked, and that repairs on his chief source of income have been estimated at forty grand. Throughout the day William will make no mention of the accident.

Suddenly he kills the motor. Waves slosh against the hull as the boat coasts a moment, then rises and rocks on the quiet swell it created.

"I was hoping he'd stop here," Senior says. "Real good flat on a slack high."

Meko: "Me, too. I was out here two days ago and found two groups of big fish. Big fish, Pa."

I rise from the cushioned seat to take the rod from its locker, take the graphite instrument from its casing, and hand the rig to Meko—"No arguments, you're up"—intending to melt into the bottom of the skiff, to do nothing but obey the first commandment in the Book of Bonefishing: Observe. Incited by some invisible atmospheric alteration, the wind is up, pushing down the horseshoe-shaped flat, making sighting more difficult. Although he is seated in the boat at roughly the level of the roughened water's surface— not standing on the bow like Meko nor perched above us on the platform like William—Senior spots each fish in sync with the working guides; my eyes are usually a moment or two behind. Just once, nearing noon, do I spot a glimmering push of water—V's of wake with shadows of fish beneath them pushing upwind, against the current—and point it out to Senior before he's identified it.

"Ah, you got me on that one!" he says. "I must have been starting my midday nap."

William's already seen the fish, though. Rest assured, unless your guide is nodding off, he will always spot the bone-fish before you do. He might not say anything about the fish, but that is only because he knows that the longer your adren-aline is pumping, the less likely you are to deliver the clinical, surgeon-cool cast required of you.

None of this is a worry with Meko, the former (current, if you ask him, since "there hasn't been another tournament since

I won eight years ago") Bahamian bonefishing grand champion who has caught thousands of bonefish, and isn't likely to get amped up about a ten-large group of four-pounders.

"I just like to hook 'em," he says. "I get that take and the first run out of them and I'm good, man."

If you gave six saxophonists the same piece—say, "Alabama" by John Coltrane—and asked them to play the solo, you would doubtless hear the same notes and melody delivered with varying degrees of artistry and flourish. The same goes for a cast like the one Meko is making: ten o'clock, eighty feet, stiff wind over his left shoulder. Scores of anglers could muster an adequate presentation here, but none would equal Meko's elegance.

He seems to slide into his back-cast, the way a salsa dancer glides away with flair from his partner as he spins her out across the floor. Behind him, in the air, the tight fly-line loop, the angler's strongest ally against the wind, snaps open and seems to hang level for a breathless moment before he hauls the line with his left hand, thrusts his body forward, and stabs the forward cast high into the air above the water so that at the end of the line and leader the fly will stop, dead, then list like an ash or an ember toward the water that absorbs it without disturbance.

The shrimp imitation could have lit closer to the bonefish's snout only if it had landed between the fish's eyes and slid down its angled forehead to the sand. The wind buffets our shirt collars, whistles around the posts holding up the platform, tosses chop against the hull—but something that resembles silence surrounds the moment. The fish stares down the fly, and Meko, like the subtlest of puppeteers, tugs ever so slightly on the fly line: it's hard to imagine he moves it more than an inch.

The fish tilts down to feed.

Once he's cinched the fly into the running fish's mouth, Meko looks back at his grandfather: "Pa, you fight this fish!"

Senior appears delighted by the offer, and stands to take the deeply bowed rod in his right hand. The rod pulses. Orange backing peels off the reel.

"Oh, that feels good," Senior says, reveling in the connection. "Very good."

BY THE TIME WE LAND THE FISH, THE WIND HAS BLOWN the skiff a long ways off the bank. Midway between two cays, the boat idles on the waves.

"Don't forget to rub the fish on the top of its head, Pa," Meko says. He smiles at me. "It makes them forget everything."

"What two cays are we floating between?" I ask.

"That's Burroughs to the left and Jacob to the right," Senior says. Thin sunlight bounces up off the waves onto his face. "One year right near Burroughs, we hooked a big fish and it ran way out there, two hundred and fifty yards. Then the backing knot broke. A day later we found the fish over by Jacob trailing backing, line, everything, and broke the fly free. Another time after a big storm I found a family stranded there. Mom, dad, two kids. Blew all the way from Abaco."

"Burroughs and Jacob—who are they named for?"

"Just a couple of guys who used to come out here a lot to fish."

"There's a Pinder's Point on the west end," William says, his voice laced with pride. "Named for Pa. Big bonefish up there."

"Must feel good to be remembered that way," I say, comprehending for the first time how far a life such as Senior's falls outside our culture's paradigm for greatness. "Whosoever will be chief among you," one teacher posed in an applicably paradoxical proverb, "shall be your servant." Naturally, like some ego-imprisoned tourist of his own experience, I begin to wonder how my descendants will remember me, but Senior rescues me from this self-absorbed state.

"Memorials are nice," he says. "But we're remembered for the lives we live every day."

Stupid Questions

Nothing whatsoever should be clung to
as "I" or "mine."
—BUDDHA

We're staked out near Lightbourne on a good tide for permit, waiting for two blacktip sharks to pass, and Merv is telling me about God:

"You know the difference between a fishing guide and God?"

"No. What's the difference?"

"God doesn't think he's God."

Tethered to its reflection on the gelatinous water, the skiff hangs in the gentle surge. A flock of small birds flies between the bow and Lightbourne.

"Merv, what kind of birds are those?"

"Caribbean doves."

"They're so tiny. Are they some special kind of dove?"

"Yeah, Caribbean."

"Merv, I'm gonna ask you another stupid question, OK?"

"OK."

"But that wasn't it."

"M-hmm."

"Kenny was trying to talk me into going to his place for dinner instead of Alma's. He said he's got the best conch fritters in McLean's Town. Where would you go?"

"That's a tough one," Merv says, making the squeaky *tsk* sound I've heard him make when I fail to spot a dubiously visible bonefish. "Kenny works full time as a mechanic, you know, and Alma works full time as a cook."

"Is that the stupidest question anyone's ever asked you on the water?"

"Not by a long shot."

"Give me a stupider one."

"Well, this one client asked me if she should stay married to her husband."

"Seriously?"

With a grunt Merv sits down atop the poling platform. He unbuttons his shirt and rolls the sleeve to his bicep and begins to scratch his inner elbow. The varnish has begun to wear off the new fiberglass push-poles, he tells me, and tiny slivers of glass have worked their way through his sleeve.

"Man, she was a curious woman. She had a real curiosity about her. All day she was asking questions, like, what's that kind of tree, what's that box-shaped fish called, what's the tide doing right now, what's—"

"Kind of like me?"

"But she was pretty. Anyway, just before lunch her husband stomps his foot on the floor, grabs her by the wrist, and says, 'Shut up, shut up, just shut the fuck up. I don't want to hear another fucking word from you for the rest of the day. Don't say another word. Is that fucking clear?' When we pull into the lunch beach, the husband, he jumps out of the boat to wade up the flat. I don't know what got between them but she stayed back and ate a salad at the picnic table. You know me, I get my sandwich down and try to nod off for a few, so I'm sleeping when she taps me with her foot. I'm like, I hope this doesn't go where I think it's going. But she kneels down in the sand and says, 'Mervin, we've been fishing together for years and I'm going to ask you a question and I want you to answer, yes or no: Do you think I should I leave my husband?'"

"What did you say?"

"I said, 'Well, how big is his big stick?'"

"You did?"

"No, man. I asked her if he said stuff like that, yelling and things, all the time, and she said not every day but almost every day. She was a little younger than him but not some championship—what do you guys call them?"

"Trophy wife?"

"Trophy wife. I told her that was too bad, but in my head I was thinking if he went after her again, I'd scrap my tip and address the situation. Sure enough we got back into the boat and I was poling and she asked, 'Mervin, do you have any idea why a skiff is called a skiff,' which is a good question really, cause I don't have any idea and I've been poling one around for thirty years. Anyway, he starts going wild on her again—'What the fuck is your fucking problem!'—and so I climb down from the platform and real easy take the push-pole, pine back in those days, and slide it between the two of them. I just nudge them apart from one another. Normally I called him by his first name but this time I said sir. 'Sir,' I said, 'you must be a very powerful man.' I let that hang in the air for a while. I picked the pole back up and pushed the skiff out a little ways from shore, let it coast. 'And I'm sure people listen to you all the time, and do what you say. But when you're speaking like that I can't hear a word you're saying. We don't talk like that on this boat.'"

"What did he say?"

"'The dock.' He said, 'The dock.'"

"That's all?"

"That's all. So I poled out to deeper water, started the motor, and headed in."

"You know I'm gonna ask you what happened next, so are you gonna wait for me to ask?"

"Look at that big bonefish," Merv says suddenly, pointing over my left shoulder at an eight-pounder the color of flint making its way over some flutings in the sand.

"Will this permit fly work?" I ask, stripping some line from the reel and readying my stance, completely abandoning Merv's story line and my plan to return serve with a story about two clients, a wildcatter from Oklahoma and his mistress, who argued so viciously one afternoon after a two-bottle lunch that the man, to quell the fight, agreed to will his mistress two wells if she would let the matter lie.

"Nah, man," Merv says. "Leave him be. We're waiting for permit. Besides, those blacktips are already on him."

Shark-loather, Merv makes his patented *tsk* sound again. I've seen him line up a hammerhead with the V-shaped prong at the end of the push-pole, the way you'd line up a pool shot, and whack the shark between its eyes. I told him what I'd read about sharks being older than dinosaurs and trees, about their olfactory lobes being able to smell prey half a mile distant, about how biologists insist the ecosystem would collapse without sharks. Merv just made his sound.

"I'm just trying to remember," he says, as if the bonefish hadn't interrupted us in the slightest, "if it was that night or the next morning that the husband's plane showed up to take her home. It must have been the next morning cause I had come to the lodge early to swap the fly rods for shark rods and she was waiting there on the dock with her suitcases by her feet. She walked right over to me and shook my hand and when she pulled her hand away there was a wad of money in mine. Tight folded bills. She thanked me, then smiled and took off her sunglasses so I could see the welt she had under her eye. Then she smiled and thanked me again."

"How much money was it?" I ask, hunching over my hands to secretly knot to my tippet Merv's favorite fly, a mantis shrimp—just in case, by Merv's fiat, we decide to slip the stake and pursue the bonefish.

"I can't say."

"You can't say because you don't remember or you can't say?"

"I can't say. There was all this stuff the workers gossiped about when they left. The wife had been flirting with another man at dinner, the husband had tried to get the masseuse to yank his cord. They were yelling at each other all night long in the cottage, he slept on the sofa in the dining room. Who can say?"

Listening to Merv, I feel three ways torn: a touch gratified that he has ventured past the typical guide-client exchange into tale telling; slightly guilty at having teased the confessional out of him, knowing from experience that an on-duty guide hypnotized by the physical motions he makes daily can become quite loose-lipped; and a bit harrowed by the narrative itself.

"It's kind of a sad story," I say. "Don't you think?"

"You love it down here, man. But it's no paradise."

"You ever been married, Merv?"

"Nah, man. By the way, I saw you put that mantis on a minute ago."

"Relationship?" I ask, looking out at a celestial mesa of cumulus that has formed to our south.

"I do have what you might call a relationship with a woman for quite some time now. When she gets lonesome, she comes over to my place. When I get lonesome, I go to hers. But I don't refer to it as a relationship."

"What do you call it?"

"I call it an arrangement."

Ennui

I offer, That hawk up there sure has it easy.
Lyle doesn't even look up . . . He says,
Easy, but hungry.

—JAMES GALVIN

Thunder runs through the dun-colored clouds running across the endlessly tall Bahamian horizon, the lightscape like a ten-mile-wide Rothko, the canvas on loan from an archangel. Free admission, today only, at the East End Archipelago Museum of Moment-to-Moment Modern Art.

Walter Reckley doesn't know who Rothko is, but he's pondered plenty of horizon. Studying the skyline, he lies on his back in the sand of Dove Cay underneath two pines the wind is having its way with, their shadows and the shadows of two scavenging turkey vultures crossing and recrossing his ample belly and round face, the ball cap balanced on his forehead shading his eyes from the sun.

He would nap, I reckon, if my puppyish line of questioning weren't keeping him awake.

"Do you think I should walk down the lee side of the island," I ask, "and look for fish?"

"Only if you feel like wasting time," Walter says without getting up. He picks up a nearby stick, breaks it, and commences rubbing the two sticks together. "Those fish are long gone to deep water with this front settling in. You might as well flip some lizards."

I stare back befuddled, an art student upon whom an allusion is lost.

"Let me see your fly rod?"

I fetch the rod from its repose against a palm trunk, and pick up my hat, in which the reel had been resting to protect the oiled gears from the sand—and hand the rig to Walter.

"You like this fly a lot?"

"No, not particularly."

"Good," he says, taking his heavy-duty fishing pliers out of their belt sheath. He snips the fly's hook off at the bend, tosses the point and barb over his shoulder into the palm grove, then peels some line from the reel and, sitting up with a groan, flicks a short cast over to the undergrowth. With his left hand, he gives the line a tug, and the hookless fly scuttles a few inches across the sand. Instantly two geckos shoot out of the weeds, stop, stare one another down with palpable feverishness, and race to within a whisker of the fly. Thin ribbon tongues sniff the air.

Quick as sin, the lizard on the right pounces on the fly, and just as quick if not quicker, Walter gives the line a tug and the rod tip a jerk, at which the small reptile goes airborne, cartwheeling through the air, then landing on its back among the wrack-line detritus of shells and dry flotsam.

It dusts itself off and attacks the fly again.

Walter tugs the fly away and laughs. "Your turn. Give it a try. Ten points for a full flip, five points if they land on their back."

It's not exactly the trough of moral turpitude, but I don't feel quite right about flipping lizards. Walter senses my hesitation.

"Come on, man. It educates them. Take a lap around the pines and see how many you can turn while we wait out the weather."

I oblige—at least Walter can knock off for a few minutes—and walk around the woods' perimeter luring geckos from the shadows, teasing them all the way to my feet. One arrives without a tail, and I admire how little time it takes for its back to morph from a banded calico to a near white, like paraffin.

Across the sand from the tailless lizard, in barely visible swarms, crickets and tiny sand fleas hop, but my fly has magnetized all reptilian attention.

It takes me a while—too long for an educated man—to parse out that flipping lizards is like dry-land bonefishing on a miniature scale, but upon returning I'm proud to tell Walter of my study.

"You think?" he says, sitting up and dusting the sand from the back of his neck. "Bones are curious creatures. Sometimes I think there's food all over the flat—shrimp and crab and perch—but they're just interested in something different, shiny. And sometimes you just flat pester them into eating your fly. Pester, pester, pester."

Walter falls back into the sand and picks up his twigs again. He strikes one stick against the other, and begins to knock out a little beat. Like many guides around here, Walter moonlights in a band.

"You practicing a riff?" I ask.

"Just a little mojo," he says. "Something to change the weather."

Resigned to the notion that our flats fishing is shot for the day, I sit down in the sand and open the lunch cooler. There is no official Bahamian guiding union that I know of, but the lunch breaks guides relish last one hour, to the minute. I've tried various methods of truncating these "union breaks"—screaming, "Shark attack!" from the water's edge, announcing the arrival of a faux school of tarpon—but they don't budge. At best they'll stir, lifting their heads from the life preservers they've been using as pillows, and talk among themselves in that rapid-fire Bahamian dialect that allows the tourist listener to distinguish only a word or two of each sentence. The cooler's contents: two ziplocked sandwiches and a bag of chips. From the treetop a pair of gulls swoops and lights near our feet.

"I got an egg salad and a turkey club. Which one do you want?"

"Oh, man, I'm good. I already ate," he says, rubbing his belly, the lower portion of which protrudes from his khaki guide shirt.

"Yeah, but which one do you want?" I'd wager my fly rod that he wants the egg salad because he's Hoovered two of them already.

"Well," he says, his voice rising, "I could do the egg salad, I guess."

"Good."

We eat in silence for a while until I ask if it gives him a sense of pride to know that he works for one of the most prestigious bonefish lodges in the world.

"Never, man. I got a lot of ways to feed my family," he says, explaining that he also fishes commercially for snapper and lobster, and repairs boat engines. "The money counts the same no matter who signs the check. People take this job too serious. I work hard, I'm good at it, guests request me. But when I'm not guiding, I don't think about guiding. At all. When I am guiding, though, it's all I think about."

A few years ago, along with another enterprising veteran guide, fed up with what he deemed unfair treatment from new management, Walter left Deep Water Cay to start a simple bonefish lodge of his own across the channel in McLean's Town. With investments from former Deep Water Cay clients, he and his partner built and assumed part ownership of the new operation. The split from Deep Water Cay was messy—numerous trips to Freeport for court hearings, threats of lawsuits, expensive legal fees, and a two-year ban from the lodge. Ultimately the new work wasn't steady enough, so Walter, chastened, went back to the well; whether he was asked back, or knocked on management's door with hat in hand, remains undisclosed.

Having experienced plenty of lows within the gimcrack world of guiding politics, I can only presume Walter didn't vault back up to the top of the lodge's totem pole.

With the sense that I'm getting to the marrow of something here, that I'm close to tapping a tender bone, I toss the crusts from my sandwich to the gulls. I've heard rumblings about the lodge's new ownership, pending changes to the operation initiated in the name of a healthier bottom line. I don't want to prod, to compromise the pride of the man I've seen stand up impromptu at Alma's diner to belt out the Bahamian national anthem, but prod I do:

"I mean, you were one of the most beloved guides at the lodge. I've met people over the years, just random people while guiding, whose faces light up at the mention of your name. But you shit-canned it?"

Walter doesn't answer right away. I suspect he is gauging his depth of reveal. *Is this guy a guide, a fisherman, or a writer?* he must wonder—the same question I have been asking myself for two decades.

"How would you feel if all of Manitoba," he finally says— "where are you from again?"

"Montana."

"How would you feel if all of Montana was owned by . . . Jamaicans? All the jobs controlled by Jamaicans? I mean, you could get a job, do good work, maybe be the best, but you could never really get over the hump because the Jamaicans owned your boats, equipment, land, all that stuff?"

I open the Lay's bag and toss a large chip to the gulls. The birds hop over and scrap for it, render it to crumbs, poke the crumbs from the sand, then look back shiftily at the Bearer of Chips.

"It would chafe me a bit," I say.

To the east the front has thinned—the bulky clouds replaced by waifs—and the blue sky above the islands looks sponged of its humidity. The air feels crisp, ten degrees cooler than it was an hour ago, a shift the bonefish likely sensed before angler and guide woke up in the morning.

Walter raises his eyebrows above his sunglasses: *A bit?*

"I guess it really would," I say, as I toss the gulls a few more chips the wind scatters across the sand.

Horizonward

Sunset is an angel weeping
Holding out a bloody sword.

—BRUCE COCKBURN

I f you believe his son William, Senior has always been a closet conservationist.

"Pa used to burn six gallons of gas to every twelve the other guides would use," William tells me as we ride his postwork ferry from the lodge to town, the bow of the laboring boat running a hawksbill turtle toward the edge of the channel. "He would pole a flat until there was no sand left to pole."

William is due to find out what repairs on his Pinder's Ferry will cost and if the party at fault—a local boater who answered his cell phone inopportunely—has current insurance to cover. In a better mood than I'd be in under such circumstances, he reaches into his shirt pocket with a wink and pulls out just the corner of some crisp bills, today's gratuity.

"He was like that about tips, too. 'It's paper,' he always said, 'and like to burn.' These boys today, they think tips are a renewable resource. Once they stop guiding they'll realize the guy putting the hundred-dollar bill in their hand at the end of the day is gonna be gone. Like he never even existed."

The lodge's ferry nudges into the dock behind William's blue-water transport, which looks to have endured something between a fender bender and an all-out wreck. I wait for William to step off and attend to his other means of living, but he nudges me with his shoulder and points out the hawksbill circling back through the channel. Sold for decades illegally to jewelry makers in Japan but now making a comeback, hawksbills are about the size of a halved basketball, and similar in color, although they move with a fluidity that belies their structure. I would swap bodies with one for an hour without negotiation, if offered the trade.

"Pa would teach the guides, unless you can handle the fish without removing its slime, don't touch it at all. Just reach down the leader and pop the hook out of its mouth. Because as soon as that slime is gone, the fish's scent starts to escape and the sharks hone in, straightaway."

Biologist Andy Danylchuk, who spent several years studying on Eleuthera, confirms the Pinders' backyard biology: bonefish subjected to gentle handling (quick retrieval, zero to fifteen seconds of air exposure) survived despite the proximity of predators, while fish subjected to rough handling (thirty to sixty seconds of air exposure) were often preyed upon by sharks or barracuda within an hour of release. Of tagged fish subjected to gentle handling, all ten remaining fish were tracked alive for at least thirteen days, suggesting that the impact of poor handling is likely to be registered within minutes of release.

Over thirty years ago, Senior helped biologists implant bonefish with transmitters for the purpose of tracking the fish's postrelease movements, and remembers finding one transmitter two miles from where they tagged the fish, he told me, "in a pile of shark feces.

"Some parts of the year they stayed real close to home, used the same flats over and over. But around the spawn, tough to track. One day they would be offshore, the next they'd be hugging the banks, the next back on the flats."

Once again Senior's decades-old observations are echoed in the most current research, only these days biologists are quick to remind us that, despite the bonefish's indisputable ecological and economic importance, fishery regulations across the Bahamian archipelago are limited. Danylchuk, with whom I've corresponded frequently, asserts that our newfound under-standing of bonefish movement and spawning aggregations has "significant implications for their conservation" since it estab-lishes that prespawn areas are located "in the transition areas between shallow coastal habitats and deep oceanic troughs, the very same places that humans find desirable for marinas and tourism development," such as Freeport, where David Junior and Jeffrey have staked their claim, or at a Deep Water Cay subject to expansion.

WITH A SETTING SUN FOR A BACKDROP AND SHINY BLACK wings spread out to dry, the cormorant perched atop an inlet buoy looks like a lanky human figure walking out of the hori-zon, pine branch yoked across his shoulders, a couple of snap-pers hanging from each end.

I'm staring out the window while on hold, waiting for Paul Adams to return to our phone conversation. Gulls fly by squawking but the cormorant does not flinch. I can hear Paul, his voice muffled, telling someone in his office that talk is cheap. The gulls orbit the buoy again but still the bird won't budge. "Words are one thing," he says. "Work's another."

"Down here in the islands," he says—and from the sudden increase in the volume of his voice I can tell he's now speaking to me again—"particularly when you're talking about money, talk is cheap."

Paul's perspective, on the other hand, is invaluable. Raised on Deep Water Cay between 1975 and 1984, when his mother and stepfather were managers there, Paul knows more about the club's third decade than nearly anyone alive, and his per-spective is singular. In the early days, Paul and his brother were the only white children at the McLean's Town school, eight and ten when they started. A lodge employee would ferry the boys across the channel to school each day, until his stepfather John Dickinson surmised that whoever shuttled them probably went home and finished a few chores before coming back to work. Dickinson soon found the boys an old fiberglass skiff, threw a four-horse motor on it, and they drove their own boat to school.

School: a cinderblock building set within a copse of trees. No power, no running water, the British teachers' thick accents absolutely inaudible if any rain fell on the tin roof or if the palm fronds scraped low in a wind above a fitful sea.

One day at lunch Paul threw up his sandwich and Senior's wife, Nicey, there dropping off food for her kids, felt his forehead with the back of her hand. "This boy isn't well enough for class," she told the teacher, and took him home, gave him some tea and toast, and he slept overnight at their house.

"That was McLean's Town race relations in a nutshell back in the late seventies," he says. "But you have to understand, I'd already lived in Exuma and Honduras. I'd already been one of the only white faces around, so I thought nothing of it. Maybe folks picked up on my nonchalance."

Perhaps the sole alienating aspect of his otherwise idyllic young life was his stepfather, who was often combative with lodge employees. The guides felt a sense of entitlement toward the motors and the boats—they spent a good deal of time maintaining the equipment—and they would borrow a transom or a gear box, loan themselves a motor when the lodge was slow, throw it on their lobster boat for a few days so they could earn some extra cash when they were out of work. They'd bring it back, of course. But Dickinson made it clear to them that the club owned everything, if not everyone, on the island.

After his brother turned fourteen and was shipped off to boarding school in Boca Raton, Paul fished the East End waters hard for a year before heading to Blair Academy in New Jersey for prep school. A decade after graduating, he was approached

by then owners Peter Pettit and Reid Sanders and asked to man-
age Deep Water. He ran the club for eight years, its salad years—
when Senior and his sons David Junior and Jeffrey anchored the
most formidable guiding lineup in the saltwater world—before
Pettit and Sanders sold to Dolan, Pollack, and Schram.

Behind their motto "Life, well played," DPS was an early
player in the "sporting club" concept, whose aim was to develop
large parcels of land into private residential "luxury colonies,"
that offered exclusive access to golf, fishing, spas, and eques-
trian opportunities. Eventual owners of Henry Ford's Savan-
nah, Georgia, retreat, West Virginia's Greenbrier Club, and the
troubled Snake River Sporting Club of Jackson Hole, as well as
other gated "outdoor pursuits" communities, DPS attempted
to expand Deep Water Cay in a similar fashion. It brokered
waterfront lots and attempted to erect vacation homes, but
sold fewer homes than lots and built far fewer homes than it
had intended.

"Deep Water Cay Club has always been unique," Paul says,
"but it's always needed money. When Gil Drake Sr. founded
the Deep Water Cay, all he wanted was a cool place to go fishing. He wasn't by any stretch a businessman. His first wife had
fronted him the money for the place, but he was so reserved. A
great guy. Deep Water Cay was his passion."

Today, Paul speaks to me from the office of the general manager at the North Riding Point Club, located halfway between
East End and Freeport, a reputable lodge in its own right and
Deep Water Cay's chief competitor. After half an hour on the
phone Paul informs me, and reminds himself, that he has some
kind of contractual gag order on matters pertaining to Deep
Water Cay's current ownership.

"Besides, my memory of the early days is shoddy at best. All
I did was fish. The guy you should really get in touch with is J.
B. Birdsall," he says.

I tell him I'm a step ahead of him, that Birdsall just a week earlier had said the guy I should "really get in touch with for perspective's sake" was Paul Adams.

Paul laughs.

It was, before all, Birdsall's uncle Jimmy Doyle, skipper of the *Heidi*, who led Gil Drake to the East End of Grand Bahama, anchoring up just off the shores of Crow Carrion now Deep Water Cay, back in 1956. Birdsall, who caught his first bonefish with Senior in 1960 and has visited the island at least once a year for half a century, contends that the club itself was on mushy financial ground quite early on. Drake had "lost most of his fortune" by the early eighties, which was why he sold. Up until the end, long after the font of his first wife's money had run dry Drake was taking money from investors, Birdsall included, and upping his own salary while making only marginal improvements on the grounds. Though Birdsall himself "put a little money in," he never thought the place could work on a reasonable basis profitwise: salt water and other elements too hard on gear; hurricanes too destructive; overhead for rebuilds too high; getting good food and booze to the end of the island too expensive.

"Birdsall told me," I tell Paul, "and I quote, 'It never was clear to me what Gil Drake's occupation was.'"

Paul laughs again and pauses for a long moment.

Just then there's a knock at Paul's office door, and Paul puts our conversation on hold again. I can hear what I assume is muffled money talk—"Two fifty now, then one hundred next week? OK, that works"—then Paul shuts the door and sighs heavily into the phone.

"Friday," I say. "Everybody wants a check?"

"No, payday is Wednesday. Friday everybody wants a loan. Gil Drake was a fisherman. That was his occupation. And as you know, dollars down here in the islands, they're a very strange thing."

THERE'S ALWAYS MONEY BEHIND THE MONEY, EVEN WHEN
the money's big. And these days the money is very big.

Paul Vahldiek is a big man with big money and even bigger money behind him. The six-foot-seven Texan and current
owner of Deep Water Cay (into which he has injected $20 mil-
lion toward refurbishment since purchasing the lodge in 2009)
was reared in Houston, the son of a butcher, next-door neighbor to Neil Armstrong. *The* Neil Armstrong. It's hard to know
whether Vahldiek's dad was a rich butcher or Neil Armstrong
a poor astronaut, but one can at least assume he came of age
among impressive stock. Now a self-proclaimed "recovering
trial lawyer," he once told a potential group of investors, "When
you grow up next to the first man to walk on the moon, nothing
seems impossible."

Nothing.

Not even amassing and owning, with a small consortium
of others (among them former Goldman Sachs general partner
David Ford), a nearly four-hundred-square-mile guest ranch
near Grand Junction, Colorado, called the High Lonesome
Ranch. A property so large that if deeded to the Department
of the Interior it would become America's twentieth-largest
national park, the High Lonesome Ranch is comprised of prodi-
gious sections of deeded and permitted lands that were accumu-
lated in part by Vahldiek's purchasing privately owned ground
that adjoined public lands, islanding previously accessible Bureau
of Land Management (BLM) tracts from the public. Owned by
some of the wealthiest people in America, the High Lonesome
"is committed to ensuring its lands, waters, and resources are
healthy and productive for compatible values and uses, demon-
strating how private and public lands can be stewarded in perpe-
tuity for ethical uses and economic vitality."

So reads the mission statement and land ethic. A land ethic that bastions large chunks of public land away from the public, and that Vahldiek apparently intends to employ as well at Deep Water Cay. "At Deep Water Cay," reads the website's "Commitment to Conservation," "we fish with an eye toward the long-term survival of bonefish." The commitment highlights a bonefish-tagging study the lodge has embarked on with the Bonefish and Tarpon Trust, an incentive-based program that involves anglers as well. "While a guest at Deep Water Cay, if you catch the bonefish with the magic tag number, you will qualify to receive a $10,000 reward. Ask a Deep Water Cay representative for more information."

At Vahldiek's Deep Water Cay, cash and conservation go hand in hand. As managing partner, Vahldiek recently called for the sale of dozens of home sites on the island (lots start at nearly half a million and fully furnished cottages are priced near $1 million), apparently engaging in a variant of the privatization model that failed previously there as recently as the early nineties. New buy-ins and the smattering of hangers-on who already own small parcels of the island will become vested members of an association and gain prioritized access to fishing dates, lodge facilities, and other perks.

Like any good owner, Vahldiek first spruced up the place. For starters, in addition to re-fleeting the lodge with a $150,000 armada of Hell's Bay skiffs, a new $40,000 Supercat dive boat, and a quarter-million-dollar blue-water vessel, Vahldiek built a new tiki bar, refurbished the lodge, hired a chef as well as a gastronomic adviser and a new marketing director, and fashioned a bona fide real estate sales department.

This high-test taste was trumped only by marketing savvy. His next moves were to remove the *Club* from *Deep Water Cay Club* and to project a spirit of inclusion through a revamped website, articles in trade magazines, and other media ventures, perhaps the pinnacle of which is the television show *Buccaneers and Bones* (sponsored by the Bonefish and Tarpon Trust, among others), which features renowned television news anchors and famous actors going after bonefish. The site's guest book now features endorsements from Academy Award winners, presidents of entertainment companies, CEOs, and other media and business luminaries. "I've seen the blueprints," one insider told me, "and Disney World has nothing on these plans."

In a dozen years, maybe fewer, Deep Water Cay could look a lot like Key Largo's über-elite Ocean Reef Club, an age-old quarter-million-dollar-a-membership club at which Vahldiek recently held a meet and greet, offering a free stay and guided fishing trip at Deep Water Cay to any Ocean Reef Club member who wished to hop a quick flight to the Bahamas and investigate real estate opportunities. Why anyone who could afford a $250,000 club membership fee, plus annual dues, would need a coupon for anything remains a mystery of the seas, but it's a fine sales technique, dished out by a salesman as shrewd as he is tall.

As a board member of Trout Unlimited's Coldwater Conservation Fund and the Bonefish and Tarpon Trust, and a founding member of the Western Landowners Alliance, Vahldiek has positioned himself as a wildlife- and land-loving tycoon with at least a modicum of science behind him. Several years ago, as CEO and president of the High Lonesome Ranch, he even founded the High Lonesome Institute, a think tank of scientists, eco-philosophers, and sportsmen established to "advance scientific and scholarly knowledge relevant to stewardship of resources on working landscapes in the Intermountain West . . . [and become] a venue for dialogue among diverse groups seeking to find common ground on conservation and sustainable development."

Nuanced as the ecosystems they affect, the High Lonesome's complicated conservation practices are understood intimately by only a few—perhaps best by former research director conservation biologist Cristina Eisenberg, who resigned from the ranch in 2012 to pursue her writing and research career at Oregon State University. Eisenberg, who remains an advisor to the operation, speaks in a video recording on the High Lonesome Ranch's website, but not before an anonymous male narrator details the ranch's "cutting-edge science" and conservation projects, which include "baseline ecological assessment of plant and animal life and . . . the health of the ranch's wide variety of animals and habitats. Objectives include improving our understanding of plants and wildlife."

Finally a shot of Eisenberg appears and she explains that the ranch is applying Aldo Leopold's land-ethic philosophy to how it manages the land, an ethic that involves living sustainably on the land, coexisting with large predators, and "utilizing resources, such as game, hunting, ranching . . . so the landscape benefits, the wildlife benefits, and humans benefit, and future generations of people benefit as well."

It all sounds wonderful, and who doesn't love Leopold, but I reckon my reservations would be tempered if I were on a high lonesome of my own, a real bender, oblivious to the fact that the "future generations" Eisenberg speaks of are most certainly the relations of those who can afford to frequent such a colossally expensive place; and if I didn't know that the powers that be at the HLR could at any time, if they so wish, begin the parcel-by-parcel sale of the property, or develop it to their own specifications; and if I weren't so pungently reminded of the embittered speaker of an old poem by William Stafford, who after a long exploration into the mountains finds himself stranded on the vast property of a famous singer: "It has been a long day, Bing," he concludes. "Wherever I go is your ranch."

The truth here, like every important truth, is complicated.

If Paul Vahldiek hadn't purchased the lands that comprise the HLR, much of the government-owned tracts would likely remain cattle-hammered, mine-shaft-shunted disgraces to land management; the truth is that Vahldiek has largely proven that for wide-scale conservation to truly take root in contemporary Western states, it must lead to some economic benefit; further, much of Vahldiek's private land purchases were from older ranchers whose own descendants either couldn't afford the inheritance taxes on the land, or might have quickly parceled up the ranches for resale; what's more, if Vahldiek hadn't kicked them off, Shell and Chevron would likely be wreaking a fracking havoc on the ecosystem and its watershed. Despite his proximity to massive wealth, Vahldiek is probably akin to the rest of us: more like a Bahama Mama (rum, coconut rum, grenadine, orange and pineapple juices, and crushed ice) than a shot of straight *añejo*.

This snippet from a Vahldiek soliloquy at a forestry conference at Utah State University should serve to illustrate the complexity of the situation and the man who admits that along with owning "such a landscape of a national park–sized scale . . . came the nightmare . . . that I needed to do right by it. A friend . . . told me once, 'Once a pig, always a pig. So don't screw it up. And remember, less is more.' Being from Texas that was hard to understand."

AT DEEP WATER CAY, VAHLDIEK AND HIS PARTNERS LIKELY pumped too much money into initial refurbishment, and now, needing to show return, are discovering what other owners have known since the lodge's inception: a fishing lodge isn't lucrative enough. Thus the addition of more family-friendly but anti-bonefish activities such as jet skiing, parasailing, and diving, thus the real estate.

But does "less is more" translate to fifty new cottages, to

hundreds of lots on a two-mile island? And if these expansive plans have been in the works all along, is the accrued "debt" just a useful excuse to make expansion "necessary"?

These are craven times, and the blood is on my hands, too. To get to and from this tiny island, I've flown thousands of miles on gas-guzzling airplanes several times. My well-planted eco-footprint isn't vanishing from the sand on the next bright wave, and yet that footprint is one set by a single angling tourist. The damage that current ownership could inflict is far more permanent in nature.

To wit, if he is truly interested in habitat and species conservation, why wouldn't Vahldiek just purchase the entire 2.2-square-mile island and lock it up to all but the wealthiest, similar to what he's done in the West?

The most reasonable answer, as is often the case in such situations, is that there is too much non-Vahldiek money on the table. Those involved in the undertaking want money made on their money. "Deep Water investors expect to break even," someone close to the undertakings told me. "Or better. The clock is ticking. They want to know when they're going to at least break even."

In the early days of the High Lonesome Ranch, "trophic cascades" were studied in depth: that is, the process by which entire biological systems suffer when apex predators are suddenly extracted from the equation. Danylchuk's studies speak frequently to bonefish populations in relation to high-end predators: without sharks, the ecosystems collapse.

Metaphorically speaking, who is the upper-echelon "predator" necessary to the survival of a decades-old institution such as Deep Water Cay? An investor-backed Paul Vahldiek? Or the angler who comes to East End every year, the same angler who would go elsewhere if Deep Water Cay were turned into a housing development, if said development and increased traffic pushed the fishery away from pressure?

Uncertainties aside, the way of life and economic vitality of a community such as McLean's Town is as fragile as the vital bonefish population, and would suffer greatly if the new incarnation of Deep Water Cay were to fail.

OVER ON ANDROS ISLAND, PRESCOTT SMITH, WHO OWNS and operates Stafford Creek Lodge, and whose father "Crazy" Charlie Smith is perhaps the Bahamas' most recognizable bonefisherman, would chafe at the "necessary shark" metaphor. Building significantly on his father's legacy, Smith has become an outspoken conservationist and advocate for Bahamian business ownership, and leads a new generation of uncompromising Bahamian bonefish guides intent on prioritizing essential habitat, making the islands less dependent on foreign investments and more staked in the invaluable resource of the flats. His historical purview has led him to believe that the Bahamian economy has for too long been dependent on a boom-and-bust financial model—from the cotton trade to the alcohol trade to resort development—and he insists there exists another, more long-term model.

Smith knows what he is up against but doesn't seem the least bit deterred by the odds. In his instructional DVD of casting techniques, he is shown casting one hundred feet of fly line while standing on the bow of a skiff speeding along at forty miles per hour. Don't let a little breeze deter you, he seems to say. Technique and determination are paramount. The founder of two organizations—the Bahamas Fly Fishing Industry Association and the Bahamas Sportfishing Conservation Association—Smith told me this over the phone:

"Real conservation is when local people are empowered through the use of their environment, earning a living in a sustainable way. If conservation is not about empowering local people, then it fails. The so-called conservation model is very phony and superficial. You might own some beautiful ecotourism lodge in the Bahamas that you can bring your friends to and they can rave about, but your real business, say, is a company that's destroying all the freshwater in India. When the locals are truly a part of the whole scenario, though, it becomes a way of life."

"In East End the locals really have no say. Where are the local people in these decisions? [Whites] basically have a certain role for blacks to play on Grand Bahama. Do me a favor and google Stafford Sands. You won't have to look very far. Here on Andros we enjoy a sense of freedom that they don't have there. My grandfather was an Irishman who married a black lady, so I always went a little against the grain. I know there's not a black person who's better than a white person, and there's no white person who's better than me. But on Grand Bahama you have people living in a state of siege. They either compromise themselves or they understand that their refusal to compromise will cost them a lot of money in the long run. It's not really any different from apartheid. They're only supposed to play a certain role. So long as you're mixing a piña colada, you know?

"Fly-fishing is our only chance to build a real democracy in the Bahamas. The fly rod is the key to open the lock to sustainable ecotourism in the country. Our wealth is right here within the green mangroves, if we keep on producing lobster, grouper, and conch. But of course we chose a development model that is all about destroying our true wealth for the pursuit of short-term gain. People aren't going to tell you that you have a gold mine until they're in control of it."

In 2012 Prescott traveled to Grand Bahama to speak out at a community meeting against Bahama Rock Limited, a subsidiary of Martin Marietta Materials, a publicly traded company that created Freeport Harbour and heads up the largest aggregate mineral-mining operation in Freeport.

One blisteringly cold Montana New Year's just before my basement pipes froze, burst, and flooded the rec room, I watched a YouTube video of Prescott's appearance, and found his rhetorical gifts as polished as his double haul. Wearing a pressed white fishing shirt complimented by a self-assured smile and standing before an audience of locals who packed the meeting room, as well as five company geologists from Martin Marietta who sat at a table on a stage behind him, Smith began:

"My name is Prescott Smith and I flew in from the island of Andros. I don't make any apologies for being a nationalist. I don't see boundaries. I don't see islands . . . and I've got a lot of relatives on Grand Bahama. But I listen to you gentlemen"—Smith is referring to the geologists, who are taking notes, removing their glasses, and rubbing their temples—"and I've been to every island in the Bahamas not once or twice. I've circled around the entire Bahamas more than fifteen times. I might look twenty"—with his rounded baby face, Prescott looks half his forty-some years—"but I'm much older than that. I go all over the Bahamas trying to train young Bahamians so that they'll become owners, using their natural environment. The information I'm going to share with you, I presented it to the entire cabinet of the Bahamas several times.

"Now, why am I in Grand Bahama? I've never met so much hostility trying to ask a few questions. I look at Grand Bahama from Google Earth and I see that you've cut straight through the island. You've destroyed billions of gallons of your freshwater lens."

By now sweat clung visibly to Smith's brow. He explained that the Bahamas contain the largest concentration of mangroves in the Western world, with Grand Bahama's groves second in size only to Andros's in this nursery system. When development destroys this nursery, the fisheries collapse on the Little Bahama Bank; and if they collapse there, all of the other resources for commercial fishing will be taxed to depletion.

"The north side of Grand Bahama is where all the mangroves are that replenish the Little Bahama Bank. So the depletion of your freshwater lens has implications beyond just your community. It affects marine life. If you pull the freshwater from under the trees that need it to drink, then your forests will disappear. If you pull the freshwater from under the trees that need it to drink, then your forests start to die on you.

"You only have four islands with pine forests. So I listen to these geologists, but you don't know about the Bahamas like I do because I am passionate about the Bahamas."

There was an audible murmur from the crowd, an *amen* of sorts that I rewound and listened to again at higher volume.

"I understand freshwater lens. I see the effects of pulling saltwater into the freshwater lens. I know what happens to the marine life when you extract the red mangroves, where the lobsters breed into the root. This is not about your company."

Here again Prescott turned to look at the geologists behind him, those who regard land as a commodity, a sure sign, in Aldo Leopold's words, of abuse.

"Many Bahamians also unfortunately have an attitude thinking [only] about today. I look at what has happened in Exuma. The Four Seasons destroyed the major freshwater lens on Exuma and now the resort is up for sale . . . I came to Grand Bahama because I am concerned about you. If the marine life collapses on Grand Bahama, it affects the entire Bahamas. Grand Bahama on the south side already have about eight places cut through the interior. You already cut up through this island. As a matter of fact, you all need to look on Google Earth and see that this entire island has been mapped out to dredge. Already. These guys may not tell you this but it's public information."

Another audible *amen* from the crowd.

"So what are you gonna do when the [inaudible] hits on the East End? And what are you gonna say to the rest of the Bahamas

when we're trusting you with the second-largest nursery system?
What are you gonna say to your children at the end of the day?"

NEARLY EVERYWHERE ONE TURNS, THE KIND OF EXPANSION
Prescott warns about seems inevitable, especially at Deep
Water Cay—but whether Paul Vahldiek will "put up a few mil-
lion dollars to train locals as bird-watching guides, or start a
scholarship fund to train kids to become kayaking guides," as
Prescott encourages, remains to be seen.

Perhaps Vahldiek will make such paradigm-altering
changes, revolutionize things. For now his expansion plan has
locals scratching their heads. It's a viable idea elsewhere, as one
lifetime local said, but "why here? I don't get it. There are no
beaches, per se. You aren't walking barefoot very far. The sailing
is mediocre, the diving is limited at best. Why not buy a piece of
land off Exuma where the trade winds blow through every day
and the beaches are all sugar sand? Why buy Deep Water Cay?"

According to a *High Country News* article by Michelle
Nijuis, Vahldiek's newspaper-heiress wife Lissa bankrolled her
husband's High Lonesome passion much as Mrs. Gil Drake
did for Gil back in 1956. And those twenty investors Vahldiek
involved with High Lonesome Ranch: ten million per. Deeper
still, the real money behind Deep Water Cay reportedly wells
up from an heiress to an Austrian medical company.

Clearly murk abounds in the proverbial water, but one
thing is clear: our creation of lodges and the infrastructure necessary to sustain such lodges has marred the same ecosystem
our beloved *Albula vulpes* requires for survival. For centuries
we pursued fish for food, but in recent decades our motivations
have become more complex, if also more than a little convoluted.
The bonefish, however, knows precisely what it wants: to stay as
far away from us as possible.

The Great Democracy of the Possible

In dreams we stand in this great democracy
of the possible.

—CORMAC MCCARTHY

The night Senior went under the knife to have his brain tumor removed, Delcina dreamed she was fishing with her father on a day so calm she could see a school of bonefish stretching from shore to horizon.

"And," she tells me, pointing out across the actual ocean and shaking her head, "I don't ever see the fish."

It's a cool evening just after sunset, and the water looks like a window filled with cerulean light but laid down horizontally, a seemingly infinite pane. Still dressed in her uniform, Delcina has just endured a long shift at the lodge but she is kinetic with story. The least fishy in a family of fishers, she possesses a memory keen as a guide's but one put to use in matters domestic. She can recall with detail, for instance, who attended Senior's bed the night before his operation, or retell the childhood story of the time one of the boys smoked marijuana and Senior's normally placid demeanor was replaced with one of rage. Well into her forties, she still calls him Daddy.

Though I have other inquiries for this gentle chronicler, we have already delved into the imaginative subconscious—where to go from there?

After dark I lie in bed listening to the palms stir and think of how rare it is, in this age of narrative dysfunction, that Delcina would want to tell her father's story more than her own. Perhaps she sees how endangered a life like her father's is, or senses that the quiet place in which his story has resided for three-quarters of a century is growing irreparably louder, and is at risk of being lost in the din. When the palms hush, I hear the distinctly feminine ocean wash across the sand, and sleepily conclude that Hemingway was only partly right: the country *was* better than the people, but not all of them.

Sometime before morning, I dream of attending Deep Water Cay's seventy-fifth anniversary celebration:

At first there is merriment, smiles, and the clinking of glasses, but then I recognize a hundred-year-old Senior there to be honored by management, walking toward me with a cane, though he doesn't regard me, or anyone that I can see, and so my dream eyes follow him through the lodge's rooms. Meko, William, Mervin, Delcina, Joseph, Linda, Jeffrey, David Junior: Senior bypasses everyone as he limps through the newly renovated building.

The main room has been scrapped and rebuilt so that it vaults a great distance out over the southern flat, and the wood floors replaced with glass. Beneath Senior's feet flow spinning drifts of sand, bubbles, shell-housed crabs, perch kicking against a flood tide. The glass floor seems to extend all the way to the setting sun.

A sudden hand on Senior's back: *We've made some changes we hope you approve of. I'm happy you've seen the Eternity Room. Like walking on water. Almost. Allow me to give you the tour?*

Through the courtyard bends a small freshwater stream in which two men wearing Gore-Tex waders kneel, casting flies for rising trout. *We call this Clear Conscience Creek. Had the trout shipped in from Idaho, cutthroats, and every hour a couple of dispensers upstream dump out tiny protein-injected mayfly-shaped marshmallows that the fish feed on for ten minutes or so. Some of the members said they just loved trout fishing too much to live down here year-round, so we brought the trout to them.*

Down near the docks the boats are filled with guides and

guests, the skiffs staked out in hundred-yard increments, plying David's favorite flat. Only no one casts, no one poles. The guests wear pairs of bulky glasses, as do the guides, who point toward a large screen that spans the flat. As if casting, the guests move their arms, as if reeling, crank their hands, even lean back as if letting a fish run. But they hold some small device, about the size of a telephone, no rod or reel.

We lost the bulk of the bonefish population when we expanded the Eternity Room, and gas prices, well, you know about gas prices, gas prices being what they were, we just decided it would be a sounder investment for us to offer what we're calling "virtual" bonefishing. The guests do actually catch "fish," per se. They have to make an accurate cast, or the motion of the cast with that handheld remote, and then they have to make the correct stripping motion at the right time, as the guide tells them to, and they do actually feel the fish when it runs. They experience everything through those glasses, which were, well, it would be a bit uncouth for me to reveal their price, but let's just say they cost a bit more than a lobster platter down at Alma's.

From the north bank David looks across the water at McLean's Town, or what used to be McLean's Town. A huge, mile-wide marina loaded to the hilt with yachts and schooners—white boats gleaming like a braiding flight of shorebirds—affronts the wayside. Gone the quay where the Pinder's Ferry docked, the fish house and Kenny's shop, the few stubborn houses that had endured the last few hurricanes. And the mangroves: gone.

Again the hand on the shoulder, this one in restraint: *David, where are you going? He's trying to get into the water—can someone help me here? We certainly don't recommend swimming, David. Did someone make sure he signed the waiver?* More words, warnings from above, but the shallow water swallows them, and soon David is swimming across the flat, subsumed by a modest school of bonefish that runs perch through the turtle grass. He whirls to his left to feed, and continues on with the others, the school's shadow moving limpidly across the sand.

Then something—a skipping, injured minnow—breaks the surface of the water and the school scatters, leaving the nearby water smoky with stirred sand. The perch dangles at eye level— kicking, kicking, almost spent—and he tips down to devour it.

He is speeding away trying to locate the school but some force pulls his head shoreward. Running, he can make out the tails of his schoolmates and the deep-blue channel; then he is flipped over and tugged in the opposite direction, pulled, jaw first, by some invisible force; suddenly he is flagging, licked, his gills working harder and harder to obtain oxygen. Then he lies on his back, staring at the sky and a sudden human hand that reaches down to grasp him by the flanks.

SURFACING TO CONSCIOUSNESS, I AWAKE NOT IN A COLD sweat but with instant recognition of how fantastical, how far-fetched, the dream seems. I sit up in bed, though, and glance out the window without my glasses on: in the predawn gray the water, as far as the uncorrected eye can see, looks like an endless plain of concrete.

FAR COUNTRY

The Hunt

Man cannot re-enter Nature except by temporarily
rehabilitating that part of himself which is still an
animal. And this . . . can be achieved only by
placing himself in relation to another animal.

—JOSÉ ORTEGA Y GASSET

Once, while hunting upland birds in far-eastern Montana,
I trailed a pheasant I could not see but sensed through a
cattail-choked coulee to the edge of a field of cut barley. The
bird's tracks and long tail had not embossed the recently fallen
snow, nor had any stray feathers come to rest. I couldn't hear
anything shuffling through the stalks, nor could I smell a
bird—I simply felt certain one hid near.

Standing at the fence line where the ground cover expired,
I looked out across the prairie, stomped a few times on the
ground, and kicked through clumps of bunchgrass, mumbling
to myself, "I know there's a bird here." But no bird flushed, so
I turned to head back across the field, resigned to the lack of
weight in my game bag.

Before I'd taken my second step, a garishly plumed rooster
pheasant flushed into the windless November sky. Too dumbfounded to shoulder my shotgun, I watched the bird slip into
the winter dusk: going, going, gone.

My mile-long walk back through the acreage was then
punctuated by an under-the-breath bipolar discussion between
the instinctual and rational brains. Throughout the conversation, the pragmatist wagered that years of hunting had led
me to expect that a hunter-, coyote-, and hawk-fearing pheasant pushed out of the comfortable confines of a cattail stand

through a thinner but more navigable sea of barley to the edge of its safe zone would have no choice but to take flight, and so it was mere logic that had preceded my prediction. But the romantic empiricist wondered if some less evolved but more attuned part of my brain hadn't indeed registered the bird's running— even though my conscious brain hadn't registered a sound—or caught a glimpse of it, or, God forbid, scented it.

It all seemed scantly plausible. What is instinct, after all, if not the reptilian brain reminding us that it's still there?

IN THOMAS MCGUANE'S NINETY-TWO IN THE SHADE, protagonist Tom Skelton, asked by his girlfriend why he's so fond of fishing, answers: "Because it's pointless and intuitive."

For millennia, pre-Skelton, the original "point" of fishing and hunting was to procure food. The hunter or angler who returned from an expedition with a story such as that of my sensed-but-unfelled pheasant would have been laughed off his campfire-side log. *Fool! You "knew" it was there and you weren't ready to shoot it!* Even now, in a fishing age dominated by conservation and catch-and-release, the grandfather holding a photo of his grandson releasing a trophy brown trout back into a river can be heard saying: "Why the hell go to all this trouble if you're just gonna throw it back?"

Life on Earth is roughly 3.5 billion years old. Onto some craniums, this factoid falls like the weight of the world; onto others it lights like a mental gnat. Regardless, Darwin would remind us that all forms of life developed from less successful forms due to genetic differences between individuals within a species. And yet: the laws of ecology and evolution no longer fully apply to us. With our catch-and-release, our hunting preserves, our stocked birds, our simulacrum canned hunts for trophy elk, we've mollified things beyond measure. True, as creatures we still operate within a trophic energy system—we eat things that have eaten things—and energy transfer can be traced to units lost during pursuit of prey and gained in consumption. But the equation has been compromised.

For nearly two million years, up until roughly a century ago, fishermen knew innately that efficient food harvest led to retention of energy, which led to a better chance of survival. The average twenty-first-century angler visiting Deep Water Cay, however, has flown hundreds of miles to Freeport, taken a cab from the airport to McLean's Town and a ferry from McLean's Town to the lodge, then motored some miles in a boat to a flat covered (he hopes) with bonefish he plans to release upon catching. The amount of individual and collective energy expended here is literally and figuratively flummoxing.

The bonefish, too, must feel flummoxed when it wanders from the safety of its school in pursuit of a crab that turns out to be a strangely textured *thing* that hooks to the roof of its mouth and tugs surface-ward. On its initial run away from the two nonstationary tree trunks (legs) or a large white mass that isn't a cloud (boat), the bonefish spends a passel of calories that would otherwise be expended during feeding or in flight from predators. It receives no essential nutrition for its efforts. Returned to the water, our fish may survive or, fight-weakened, be eaten by an opportunistic shark or barracuda, or be otherwise less able to outcompete its schoolmates for food. Such ends are discussed on a scholarly basis in papers titled *Chemical excretions of angled bonefish* Abula vulpes *and their potential use as predation cues by juvenile lemon sharks* and things of that ilk.

Though bonefish anglers don't predate like the flats' true hunters, they are more than taken by the required visual elements of the hunt: the spot of a well-camouflaged animal, the stalk on an incredibly skittish creature, the fleeting "shot" one is afforded under typical conditions. This no-blood-on-our-hands hunting differs of course from traditional methods in that the "Maker" a bonefish meets at the end of the fishing line is not a gaff-holding carnivore, but an angler clad in quick-dry clothing, who, after posing for some photos and kissing the befuddled fish's nose, sets her quarry back in the water and celebrates its dash for safe cover.

In his memoir *Meat Eater*, modern-day hunter-gatherer Steven Rinella engages this paradox in a chapter called "Playing with Food," about angling for bonefish in the Yucatan:

> One of the things I thought about was whether [my brother] Danny and I were completely nuts for spending a month camping in the sand while trying to catch a fish that we didn't want to eat. I tried to think of similar behaviors, like the way people will travel halfway around the world just to look at a piece of art . . . but . . . we weren't just coming to look at bonefish. We were coming to catch them and touch them as well. It was more like traveling around the world in order to scratch a mark into a painting and then buff the mark away.

How would the bonefish's existence differ, one wonders, had it not been discovered as a sport fish and risen into the rarified air of resource? It's speculation—for what would we use gold if we hadn't decided to trade it as currency and encircle our fingers with it?—but safe to say the bonefish would continue to annoy the commercial fishermen into whose nets it often finds its way. Natives and locals throughout the Caribbean would still utilize the bone as a subsistence fish when more desirable species such as snapper and grouper weren't available, but this is the upside. In the worst of worlds, harvested bonefish might be ground up into dog food or lawn fertilizer, the fate of fish considered "undesirable" by the commercial industry.

Instead the glorified minnow has evolved into a conservation emissary. To speak practically, many conservationists argue that great fisheries and game populations will survive only if great habitat is preserved. And such habitat will not be preserved unless the people who might otherwise develop it stumble upon a tangible reason—the knuckle-busting run of a bonefish, the rattling gills of a leaping tarpon, the shining scimitar tail of a feeding permit, the snot-spraying, high-pitched bugle of a elk, the covey flush of a sharp-tailed grouse—to do so.

Consequently, the best anglers and hunters usually evolve into the most passionate stewards of the land. A first-time Montana elk hunter, for instance, doesn't drive to his local sporting-goods store, buy a license, a .30-06, a sleeve of 180-grain bullets, and some blaze orange, drive to a random spot on the map in the mountains, step out of the pickup, and shoot an elk. Preparation includes logging long hours of scouting, stalking, map studying, and wrong turns. This prehunt penance usually leads the hunter deeper into the woods and closer to his food source to discover that his desired quarry requires for its survival a certain type of wild terrain that precludes development and infrastructure—a quality of life, if you will. It doesn't take most hunters long to figure out that the wrong votes and campaign contributions will tame this necessary wilderness more quickly than a boot-snapped twig will spook an elk. This relationship is complemented by what one of our more mindful hunters, Aldo Leopold, concluded: that in addition to engaging more deeply with their food source, hunters actually help maintain the health of game populations by culling weaker members of the herds.

To hunt anything—game animals, morels, antler sheds, huckleberries—is to abjure commonplace diversions and dedicate oneself to the occupation of being creaturely. And death, that grounding consequence for all creatures, is often the ultimate requirement of the hunt.

After an arduous twelve-mile hike on a rancher's land during which I failed to shoot the aforementioned pheasant, I returned to the homestead with a mere Hungarian partridge to offer the proprietress. "Nice going," she said, holding two sharptails she'd shot from her back porch while I was gone. "That and another elk and you'll be set for the winter."

In contrast, the lack of practicality that goes hand in hand with sight-fishing for bonefish translates to a sort of purity, possibility. Perhaps the heart of bonefishing is ecstatic, more like prayer, which makes the elusive fish a grace we intuit or perhaps even glimpse at the verge of sight, then probe toward via the faith we place in the cast. After we catch the fish and hold its pulsing form briefly in our hands, we typically release it, since grace isn't edible or own-able.

Yet grace is palpable, even when it resides beyond our earthly senses.

SHARKS, I LEARNED TODAY, HAVE TINY OPENINGS IN THE skin above their mouths, extremely sensitive openings that can distinguish the electrical fields that surround all creatures. Helping to compensate for undeveloped lateral lines, these ampullae of Lorenzini allow sharks to recognize pressure a thousand times more faint than that detectable by any other group of animals. Few people alive today have attuned themselves for an entire lifetime to a single creature the way Senior has attuned himself to the bonefish; lacking fins and gills, he seems to have developed, or retained, some equivalent to the shark's detection system, something that hasn't stuck, evolutionarily, in most of us.

As for survival, not too many pictures of Senior have endured the decades, but I have borrowed a few that remain from the dining room walls of the lodge, and, wind-thinned from a day on the boat, I leaf through them with him in his living room. I feel like an obnoxious detective: *Do you recognize this man?* One image shows him wearing a wool Kangol with his well-chewed pipe between his teeth, holding, like a puppet cut out of a paper bag, the head of what had previously been a five-foot barracuda. "The shark got four feet of that 'cuda in one swipe," Senior says with audible reverence for the ecosystem's predatory hierarchy. "Big shark. Big lemon."

Flip through a dozen dated photo albums at the club and you'll mostly see shots of sunburned men with cigars in their mouths, holding dead bonefish or permit. Only occasionally does a guide—Senior, David Junior, Jeffrey, Walter—appear grasping the trophy fish by the gills, the happy guest's arm draped around the hero guide's shoulder. But these captured, sun-faded moments stand removed from the fluid tide of time. The real stories remain in the mortar of Deep Water Cay, securing the stones—actual and metaphorical—that Senior set in place over five decades ago.

Senior's own living room walls are decorated with school photos of his children that appear to have been taken no later than 1985: Coke-bottle glasses and gaudy collars snapped up, paisley-print shirts and high-top fade hairdos. Not dated, however, is the new Dell computer against the wall at which Senior's teenage grandson Jason is tapping, placing photos on Facebook, I assume, updating his status. The look on Senior's face says, *What else?*

"He's real good at the computer," Senior says.

Jason is in eighth grade and he's a big boy, might have a future in sports.

I look over at the young man hunched in front of the screen, then back at Senior. "You think he might ever take up guiding?"

Senior says nothing, though he emits something resembling a grunt.

"Meko's son is only six years old but they're getting him on the water, catching fish." Senior flicks the fringe of the white curtain covering the window. The curtain is embroidered with roses, deep magenta, that match the color of the velour couch.

"When you guided, did you ever get the sense that you were doing good work? I mean, beyond taking a couple of sports fishing for the day? What was your mission out there, aside from catching fish?"

"Normally when I get out there on the water I start to think about my soul." He says the word—*soul*—without a shred of self-consciousness. It sounds radical when used without irony or qualification. "The fishing was a way of getting people to feel more than the fish on the end of their line. The guests were always much more educated than I am but they had misunderstood some of the principles of their life."

At the computer Jason straightens briefly, then slumps over again to attend to a video game that has him in its grips.

"One day I had taken some guests out to the Cross Cays and was starting back for the lodge when the motor gave out. I had to pole over fifteen miles back to the lodge. We slipped through the smallest creeks. Those are my favorite places, the little lagoons that run through the mangroves. I told the guests not to worry, that we could eat conch and fish if we had to sleep out, but near dusk the water started to glow with phosphorescence. There was some commotion out in the channel, water thrashing everywhere: a hammerhead, about fifteen feet long, attacking a lemon shark as long as the boat was wide.

"Those men got real quiet. By the time we got home, Mr. Drake was pacing up and down the dock, shaking the ice in the bottom of his glass. The guests looked like ghosts. But they both thanked me. One of the men wrote me a letter a lot of years later, to say he still hadn't forgotten about it."

So do you think there's a next generation? I ask. You think the kids will actually go fishing, not just play video games about going fishing?

"Well, sir"—Senior looks over at Jason, who hasn't once in the past twenty minutes turned to regard us—"I hold out hope."

SENIOR SHOWS ME TO THE DOOR. OUTSIDE THE DARKENED kitchen, over the yard and the junked cars in the yard and the palms and pines surrounding the yard, over the mangroves and shacks and moored boats down at the water, there remains the slightest remnant of the blue hour, palest of blues fading into black—and then, like that, the first star appears, white as a shark tooth. My pace quickens as I imagine the wakes of those two predators emerging under Senior's boat, their slick bodies blasting through the surface, the water afroth with blood. I think of Senior all those years ago, pecking his way with the pole across the bottom whose contours had vanished into shadow, aware that a stray gust of wind could put him out in the Northwest Channel, adrift on the Tongue, at the mercy of the currents.

Chance Baptisms

It is not down on any map; true places never are.

"Dad, what does water taste like?" asked Luca, three years old and having already found a koan to last a lifetime.

"I don't know," I said, putting out his bedroom light. "I guess that depends on what was last in your mouth. Or what kind of cup you drink it out of. Or the tap. Or the well. It depends on a lot of things."

"If you don't know, you can just say."

"OK, I don't know."

"You could tell me a story then?"

This was the winter of 2007, late in that seemingly end-less, claustrophobically gray season that would not give way to spring. Even as the days lengthened, I found myself tick-gripped by depression, a complicated clinical mind state not assuaged by the weather, the inevitable uncertainties of parenthood, or my tenuous state of employment coupled with what dregs of dollars remained in our bank account at the end of each month.

But I loved putting my boy to bed at night.

All afternoon the snow had shaded off to sleet, which had shaded off to rain, which had grown so warm—the scent of the ocean in it?—that by nightfall the foot of drift on the roof had been reincarnated as a steeply sloped river channeled through gutters. Water coursed through the aluminum, and I listened with deep intention to what sounded like clemency.

"Dad, tell a story," Luca said. "Tell my favorite."

"OK," I said. "'Little Bear's Big Fish,' by Luca and Dad."

To summarize—sans the creaking bed and delectably warm

accompaniment of a just-bathed boy—"Little Bear's Big Fish"
is the tale of Little Bear, who usually accompanies his father
Big Bear on fishing trips, but one day decides to go fishing on
his own. All goes swimmingly on this particular summer day
until Little Bear, who simply desires one modest fish for dinner,
hooks a small trout that is eaten by a middling trout that is sub-
sequently eaten by a large trout, this last fish larger than any Little Bear has ever seen: the Hawg of Huckleberry Creek! After
some fancy rod-handling and a deal brokered with the Lady of
the Creek, the invisible governess of the waterway—"If you help
me land this fish, I promise to release all fish that I catch forever"—Little Bear beaches the lunker, and offers a deal to the
fish: I will let you go, if you let the fish in your gullet go, and
that fish must in turn release the fish I hooked first. Reluctantly
the Hawg caves, but says it can speak only for itself, and that
the middling fish must give up the little fish of its own accord.
And so Little Bear must stick his head deep into the dark maw
of the Hawg and offer a second deal to the middle fish. He is a
long while in the damp echoing cavern of the fish's mouth negotiating, but the deal is ultimately accepted—though only on the
condition that this tale of fish-on-fish mercy be kept secret for
time immemorial. If the story is ever told or even alluded to, the
middle fish says, the Lady of the Creek will be alerted, and all of
your future fishing will be cursed with an empty creel.

What is Little Bear to say? Of course he accepts, puts his
rod under his arm, and begins the long walk home, during which
he is by turns aglow with having caught the Hawg of Huckleberry Creek and despondent at having to keep his tale under
wraps. By the time Little Bear reaches the cabin, it is late and
his parents Big Bear and Middle Bear pace the front porch with
worry. Welcoming him with hugs, they note his eyes a-brim
with story and beg him to tell them what happened. In truth, he
says, I got one bite. Surely there's more to it than that, Big Bear

says, winking. I have the pan sizzling with butter and garlic and lemon, says Middle Bear, peeking into his creel. But Little Bear holds firm, keeps his eyes to the floor, and enters the strangely lit room reserved for those who are witness to the miraculous.

I don't know exactly when my young listener nodded off, but when I finished my story I looked down at his head to find his large brown eyes shut, his eyelashes twitching. I listened to his breathing, to the sound of the melt charging off the roof, and closed my eyes as well. I stood up out of bed and gently tousled his thatch of hair—barely wet—then walked down the dark hall, a scant dampness on my palm. A hint of the Absolute, perhaps, or the hint of a hint we carry within our earthly bodies.

Had Luca not fallen so easily asleep, I might have segued into a tale of my childhood river, the Red Cedar, which many locals called the "Red Sewer" for the abundance of shopping carts, diapers, and condoms found peppering its banks. The young reverent trio of musketeer anglers I grew up a part of refused to defame the river with such a moniker, but we didn't ignore the trash; to the contrary we embraced it, named the eddy behind the pile of shopping carts the K-Mart Hole, called the gravel bar near which we'd weekly discover a discarded condom or two the Spawning Bed—to be precise, it was the most sexually and ironically advanced member of our crew, Kobi Hatcher, who mused up that nickname.

Kobi was also the most refined fisherman. From the polluted Red Cedar, Kobi caught and showed Jomo Grady and me how to catch smallmouth bass, largemouth bass, rock bass, walleye, pike, a tiger muskellunge, Skamania steelhead, even salmon. Kobi reveled in the ridicule he received from college students lugging their textbooks across the bridges under which we fished: "Caught any diapers today?" they'd

yell, and Kobi would shoot a smile up at them before hooking another scrappy bass. We fished roughly fifteen miles of
the Red Cedar, from Lansing, where it wove between General Motors plants, through the university campus in East
Lansing and out to suburban Okemos, where our best hole
bordered a country club golf course and required stealthy
trespass to reach.

On a Michigan State football Saturday once, armed with
his light-tackle smallmouth gear and a three-inch plug, Kobi
hooked a startlingly large male coho salmon at the base of
the bridge pool. Beer-rowdied, posttailgate football fans on
their way to the gridiron soon became spectators to the battle
between young man and fish. Fighting the twenty-some-pound
prespawn fish on four-pound test and limber six-foot rod, Kobi
couldn't exactly order the fish around, and so the group of
gapers soon grew to a bona fide congregation. Several times
the fish ripped a ream of thin monofilament off the reel, then
leaped free of the water, shattering the otherwise glassy pool,
the crowd gasping as it would later for a bone-jarring tackle or
a one-handed touchdown grab. Though the light tackle should
never have allowed Kobi to bring the heavy fish to shore, he
nagged it there with the subtlest of pressures, urging it to the
shallows, where I clasped my right hand around its forearm-
thick tail.

Dripping, ripe with spawning colors, heavy as an anvil,
the fish seemed forged, pulled, an instant before, from the fire.
Resting the fish beneath the river's translucent surface skin so
it could breathe, I read apathy in its eyes, and apathetic was
the angler to the shouts of his temporary acolytes: "What'd
you get it on?" "Are you going to keep it?" Kobi reached his
fingers into the thorny kiped jaws of the salmon and rattled
the treble hooks free. Then he took the fish from me, lifted
it dripping into the chill October air for one elastic moment

before submersing it again in its domain: one tail thrust, and it disappeared from sight.

What does the holder of a moment hold when the moment is gone? After the water turned wine's been drunk from the cup, what remains? And the miracle maker, what does he say after the bread's been multiplied? Nothing. For a long, long while. And then, if the miracle maker's sixteen, and has just transfigured a mammoth salmon from a body of water most people wouldn't have deigned to spit in: "Let's go call our girlfriends and see whose parents are gone for the afternoon."

"There are no unsacred places," Wendell Berry writes, "there are only sacred places and desecrated places." Desecrated, no doubt: Kobi's ticketless fans dropped their beer cups into the Red Cedar after the show had ended. And though I had no idea back then, I had witnessed the fusing of two seemingly unconnected worlds, the vile and the pure, and the sacredness of a place—the base of that pool at the head of that rapid—had been born in me.

"AT THAT TIME," SENIOR SAYS FROM THE STERN OF HIS BOAT, "darkness was on the face of the deep."

It's a few minutes before five a.m., a few hours before sunrise. I hear the soft hiss of sand against boat hull as Senior beaches the Carolina skiff on the Deep Water side of the channel. Dead low tide. He notches a sputtering propane lantern to the tip of his push-pole, leans starboard, and sweeps the lantern above the water like a priest swinging a censer. Like smoke the light spreads across the water's misty surface. He holds the lantern still, and its beam augers a bright-yellow hole in the shallows, splintering a school of perch. He hands me a bucket, and motions for me to step ashore.

"The Lord spoke and said 'Let the dark be divided from the

light. Let dry land appear.' So we know that the water was here even longer than the land."

Although the water must have rested on some landform, I think, been held by some type of earth. That is, the water wasn't just washing through space. How I've gone from checking Senior's lobster honey holes to delving the early shifts of the Devonian era, I'm not sure. I think to ask him, but there's a sudden bump against my calf: just the nearly beached buoy marking Senior's spot.

"Let there be light on my lobsters," he says, handing me the lantern. "And let these lobsters be slow."

I cast the light over his shoulder as he probes the seafloor with the tip of his push pole, his steps announced only by the water falling from his pant cuffs back into itself.

"There's a plateful," he says, and there, netherworldly in the lantern's milky cast, are three Caribbean lobsters cramped in a gnarled basalt pothole, their beady eyes strangely vacant in the light. Senior pins one to the bottom with the pole and grabs the other two in his right hand, the harvested rusty-black crustaceans clacking against each other, their long antennae waving. He releases his grip on their upper abdomens and tosses them into the high-walled bucket, where they scramble against the plastic bottom and one another.

"Take the other and put a little water on them. There are usually some giants on this bank, big ones come up out of the blue hole."

I set the bucket down and reach to grab the lobster between its carapace and tail—I know these Caribbean lobsters don't have pincers like Atlantic lobsters or the crawfish I caught in Michigan as a kid, but I'm skittish nonetheless—then lose hold of the lantern, which submerges in the water with a pitiful whisper.

"I'll get it," Senior says, chuckling.

"Wait, I see it," I say, though I don't see anything. I plunge my hand into the water and wave it back and forth through the shallow blackness, certain a shark will have it. My fingers nudge something metallic, then something glassy, and then I have the handle and am pulling the water-filled lantern up from the not-so-deep depths.

"While you're soaked," Senior says, "how about some water in this bucket."

My sweatshirt sleeve is drenched to the armpit. We'll harvest no more lobsters, and Senior will have to pole us home in the dark. Though we're not even a mile from the docks, and the tide will carry us quickly, it's an inconvenience, and a truncated harvest, to say the least.

"I'm sorry about the lantern. Stupid."

"Oh my. It's not a problem, sir! We'll make it home easy. With my eyes closed."

The gentlest thing in the world overrides the coarsest, I think, cribbing loosely from the Tao. Nothing in the world is weaker than water, but it has no better in overcoming the hard.

Soon we're gliding back across the channel through the cooling air. Though I can't see much, I close my eyes anyway and listen to the three precious culinary centerpieces-to-be sloshing in the bucket, to the push-pole sliding in and out of the water, and, farther out, to the peepers and night frogs in metallic chorus. Occasionally a heron senses our presence and squawks out the equivalent of a belch at a meditation temple.

Senior clears his throat.

"They didn't always used to have lanterns on lobster boats, either."

"What did they use?"

"Pine torch."

A WIND OF GOD HOVERED OVER THE WATERS.

The waters saw you, O God.

Invoking angels, ancient Jews wore white and immersed themselves in the river every day, eighty days, every evening and morning, in places that were hidden from people. Some rabbis felt that the divine name should be transmitted from one person to another only over water.

He will lead them to springs of living water and the Word would come to them—to Ezekiel by the river Kebar. To Daniel by the Tigris and the Ulai. Jacob by the Jabbok.

Places of beauty, I can only assume.

Perhaps, but *what is beauty if not the beginning of terror?* (Rainer Maria Rilke)

The Great Flood is the means by which God undoes the cosmos.

The primordial soup of creation.

Before the child can be born and the parents' cosmos come undone, the mother's waters must be broken. A child born directly into water such as a warm birthing pool can breathe fully submerged, for minutes, with its eyes wide open, arms turning like fins, its body still capable of siphoning oxygen from fluid.

A bath when you're born, a bath when you die—that's all. (Kobayashi Issa)

When the Hindu gods wished to squelch an uprising of nongods, they enlisted the sage Agastya, who was only the size of a thumb but powerful enough that when he drank up a handful of water, all the oceans of the world dried up, allowing the gods to vanquish their foes.

"No matter what the obstacles," an old mountain recluse observed, "water reaches its goal, whether by uniting with the air and getting a free ride, or by skirting around things or patiently eroding them. Consider how marvelously it blends all things to its purposes; voiceless, it generates sound both musical and thunderous by context with the other elements; tasteless, it conveys all tastes and odors; colorless, it reflects all hues. It demonstrates that there are peaceful ways of solving all problems, accomplishing all ends."

Truth is compared in scripture to a streaming fountain; if her waters flow not in a perpetual progression, they sicken into a muddy pool of conformity and tradition. (John Milton)

The great Tao flows everywhere, to the left and to the right. All things depend on it to exist and it does not abandon them. (Lao Tzu)

Whatever is sacred, it is a flowing. (Rumi)

The world of dew is the world of dew—and yet, and yet. (Kobayashi Issa)

We breathe it, we drink it, we spit it when we speak. Salty, it falls from the corners of our eyes and dampens our handkerchiefs. It drips from our pores when we run, when we pole a skiff, when we make love. The moisture in the air we breathe (one-third of all the water in our bodies comes from inhalations) contains the exhalations of others, our enemies, our friends, the creatures four-legged and winged, and marries itself with the water the body contains. Verily, verily, the science of physics says: we are one water.

The brain needs the viscosity of cerebrospinal fluid to function.

Tears are liquefied brain. (Samuel Beckett)

Scientist Peter Marshall:

The ability of water to absorb large amounts of energy buffers photosynthesis in cytoplasm and the transfer of oxygen in animal blood from chaotic flux; moderates the Earth's climate by using oceans and lakes for heat storage; eases seasonal change and our body's adaptation to it by slowing, without shocks, the change of weather. . . .

Most of all, water's specific . . . heat of fusion gives life its ability to maintain in hard times. Without these molecular traits, climatic extremes would turn living creatures over to their Maker at unprecedented rates.

Translated: When we run hot water on our hands and feel the warmth in the back of our neck, it's because of the water in our body, what C. Scott Ryan calls "the literal river beneath our skin."

Whether pond, river, puddle, lake, sea, or cloud in reflection; whether warm as the quilt a mother drapes over a sleeping child, or cold as a burial sheet—we can't help but bow to it.

Of Principles

Water is earth's eye.

—HENRY DAVID THOREAU

Because I'm often mistrustful of my own motives, my so-called plans and their execution, I prefer to rely on reaction, on readiness of mind when it's available. When I first met Senior, I had no inkling that his life would affect my worldview so thoroughly, and this is doubtless for the better. Had I sensed the size and rarity of the fish, I suspect, I would have botched the cast.

I've awoken early, but spend a while shaking off the previous night's dinner, Senior's favorite: turtle soup. In the rich salty broth floated chunks of potatoes, carrots, and turtle meat of two different textures—one that resembled lamb or brisket, and the other, from the more tensile belly of the turtle, that tasted slightly feral, forbidden.

Where the turtle came from and how it was killed no one at the table would say. It was likely spotted by a fisherman who revved up his outboard and chased down the fleeing creature, then netted it or stabbed it with a long-handled gaff. A lodge guest requested turtle soup, but, bound by regulations, the kitchen there won't serve turtle. Across the channel, however, Alma was happy to oblige. She cooks what meat they bring her.

While ladling me a second portion, Senior said they used to run the hawksbills down with the motor and jump on them, an image that would reconstitute itself in my consciousness in the following hours.

I loaded my spoon with meat that recalled, in appearance, one of my grandmother's pot roasts, and tasted good, tasted fine.

I considered the countless varieties of wild game I've enjoyed over the years, everything from elk heart to mountain goat sausage to squirrel hasenpfeffer—but something about the turtle made me squeamish. Big medicine.

Later I dreamed vivid turtle dreams. First my bare chest was wrapped tight to the armored carapace of a gaff-fleeing green turtle, my arms wrapped around its shell, its flippers spinning frantically: a few seconds of appropriated flight, the water and weeds rushing by my face. Then I was what I had eaten, a turtle fleeing the flat, my carapace flipped vertically so as to evade a shark's open-but-not-wide-enough-to-take-my-canted-shell mouth—and was not the least bit enamored of my transformation.

Not far off the wayside, the shallows are creature-stirred this morning. I half expect a turtle to ghost up out of the refraction and regard me, but it's a gathering of bonefish plumbing the shallows. The school numbers a dozen, and each member is a close-to-double-digit bruiser, broad, snubbed off like a revolver round. Above, somewhere between the top of my head and the firmament, unseen birds whirl by. The poet in me thinks there is no need to fish: just revel in this scene. Then, up from the water, like a slack flag lagging in a lee, another bright, dripping tail that looks ten inches tall, and I hear the hunter in me, saying, *You could rig your rod in ninety seconds, roll your pants up, wade up to your ankles, and have a pretty good shot at these fish, these big fish.*

In no time—Clark Kent in the phone booth—I am at the ready, hat on, rod rigged, but my fingers shake as I fumble through my backpack for my fly box, then through the fly box for a shrimp imitation. Why anyone would ever want to become surgeon-cool at this—to be able to tie, without quaking hands, an improved-clinch knot to the eye of a hook—is beyond me. My fumbling fingers assure me: I am alive on this ground of many gifts.

Slipping into the water, I peel fifty feet of line from the reel, and from the tip of a nearby pine, a kingfisher acknowledges the reel gears' racket with its maniacal laugh. The bones acknowledge my presence as well, not spooking the way a school of lesser fish would, but angling off so that they're just vaguely out of range: as if both man and fish were magnets. I've seen big white-tail bucks use this same evasive tactic—*I'm not going to bolt,* they seem to say, *'cause that would use up too much energy, but I'm going to keep working my way toward the door, in case I need to slam it in your face.*

After a few minutes, the fish are milling around unworriedly again—I count six tails at once—with eyes focused on the bottom. They are about a cast and a half away. I'll have to wade out to my waist to reach them. It's either that, I think, or wish all Montana winter that you had.

TEN MINUTES LATER I'M RELEASING A REGAL CREATURE, a nine-pound bonefish, my biggest of the trip, back into the still-falling tide. I hold the fish under the water and stare into its eyes, which are bright with its purpose: survival. I let go of its tail and it shoots across the shallows and over the bank into the unseen.

Waist deep, I am returned to the principles Senior referenced without elaboration the other evening: "Fishing returns a man to his principles." Over a lifetime of fishing I've learned that attentiveness is the first of these. When we attend thoroughly to our surroundings, we enter the prayerful closet of the senses and close the door.

Above me the faint moon, the cuticle of a god, vanishes into blue sky. "Beautiful," I whisper to myself as it goes, and mean it, and know it. Appreciation, then, is a natural aggregate of the angling experience, integral to our being, and another of

Senior's fundamentals. Sheer curiosity at the polyclad, the flat-worm that looks like an underwater monarch butterfly! Baffled joy for the feather duster whose parakeet-like crown is an areole positioned to sift food particles from seawater!

I drag my left hand in the water as I walk shoreward, aware of the distressed-bonefish scent I trail as I go. A few small bon-nethead sharks circumnavigate the flat, no doubt aware, in their sensory organs at least, of the fish I just released, but I sense no threat from their presence at the flat's periphery. A friend told me once of crouching down in a catcher's stance to release a small bonefish only to watch a three-foot blacktip race through his legs to take the bone in its maw a split second after the fish was freed. The sudden vividness of this story has me high-stepping it to dry land. Pulse-quickening wonder at the creature world: Senior's third principle.

If attentiveness leads to gratitude, and gratitude to "rever-ence," as Milton had it, then perhaps reverence leads to mystery, which wends toward a deepening of our precious but treacher-ous relationship with Earth, this palace of ordinary people.

Once, at sunset, trying to comprehend the bonefish's feed-ing habits, I slipped into shallows that scarcely covered my back, closed my eyes, and began to plumb the flat with my lips. How soft the earth's kiss, I thought, pressing my face into the ash-like oolitic particulate. Then I felt something sharp flick against my face, and surfaced with a gasp, fearing my lips had found a crab: just a mangrove twig, and the blunt reminder that I no longer forage live crustaceans, nor flee toothy predators.

Thumb and cranium have carried us a long way—arguably too far. Collectively we upright mammals appear incapable of viewing water as we eons ago viewed it, as the fishes view it now: as an element that binds us each to each, and upon whose flour-ishing we depend. Though this is far more than an actualized man such as Senior would care to articulate.

THE BLUE HOLE—AN UNDERWATER CAVE THIRTY-SOME FEET in diameter and twice as deep—stares up from the flat like a massive sapphirine pupil. If colors are, as Goethe said, the deeds and sufferings of light, then light here is perpetually afflicted.

Charged with catching dinner, Senior and I have caught enough and now we're simply looking, gazing with something resembling reverence into the seemingly bottomless, flooded, spring-fed cave that has deepened into the limestone after eons of rotating sand and retreating ocean currents. Within a twenty-mile radius, depending on tides, over a dozen such holes boil up or flush down from the old seafloor through which time has eaten, creating a maze of subterranean freshwater rivers.

Senior jigs his hand-line rig and says his mother often warned the children about diving into blue holes. Not a chance, I agree, while reeling up my sinker, hook, and hunk of perch tail, not for a million bucks would I swim down there. Senior gives his hand-line a little tug. What Jonah-swallowing denizen of a jewfish, I wonder, lives down there?

I recall reading an article on the plane trip down, some airline rag, that said the caves contain sulfur, too, and that the Lucayans used to dive to their deaths in blue holes. As the boat's bow yaws across the opening, phrases like *hydrogen sulfide* and *inevitable delirium* come to mind, also that the skulls of natives, gifted divers who were forced by invading Spaniards to gather pearls, had additional bone near the ears due to the buildup of brain pressure. Skilled teams of archeologists and scuba divers have discovered burial (or perhaps sacrifice, or even mass suicide) sites of Lucayans in blue holes. The unique water chemistry of the caves preserves bones and even soft tissues for thousands of years, making the holes in the Bahamas veritable ossuaries of humans, crocodiles, tortoises, bats, and owls.

Tortoise shells thousands of years old, tissues preserved. Leaves that still possess their structure and pigments, and insect wings that still shine with iridescence.

Compromised by rising sea levels triggered by climate change, the delicate water chemistry of these caves remains under constant threat. They are so chemically distinct that when scientists analyzed the DNA of microbes from five inland blue holes, no shared species were found. Stranger yet: some of the organisms in the caves use energy-harvesting methods scientists previously thought impossible. All the little live things imprinted with their own dynamic identity, what Gerard Manley Hopkins called "inscape."

Though the human is the most "highly selved" of things, the most distinctive being in the human-known universe, animals, plants, and even places elicit what Hopkins called "instress," that intense thrust of energy that enables one to realize one's own specific sanctity, the stamp of divine creation, if you will. The Word, Senior might say, that was with all things in the beginning.

I ponder all of this somewhat fugally as we drift in the skiff across the threshold where the porous limestone floor drops from three to thirty feet. From the bow I can't take my eyes from the round liquid jewel. Topaz, emerald, aquamarine: the high sun has turned the surrounding flat into a beveled tray of gems. We are charged with water's grandeur. True, it mesmerizes, enraptures, haunts; but gazing into it one also recognizes, somewhere very deep in one's core, that of which one is made, an element full of fluidity and possibility, and, quickened by this realization, one aspires to these qualities.

I look over at Senior, at the tight but untwitching line that runs from the coil in his hand to the bottom of the hole. I want to give form to my ruminations, ask him if he understands, but I realize he would probably just nod politely and say, "Yessir," so I offer:

"You seem happy."

"Oh, yessir."

"Do you worry about anything?"

"No sir, not a thing."

Too often my own worry has seemed a constant companion, but water has often righted me. During times of emotional difficulty I have tended to "self-medicate," to seek out water not simply to fish but to listen to, or even immerse myself in. Near our home in Montana there runs a small creek, and upon occasion, sometimes in the throes of dread, I have found myself on a bridge above this creek, standing parallel to the downstream rush, imagining the water coursing through my head, ear to ear, flushing out the worthless sediment of angst.

A few Julys ago, I floated a man and his teenage foster son down the Bitterroot River. The man obsessed over catching trout on a fly rod, but the son preferred to dangle his feet over the side of the raft or, when the boat was banked, sit on the warm streambed with his legs immersed in the cold clear flow. Eventually I asked if his feet weren't getting cold, if he didn't want to explore an island or try landing a fish. "Thanks," he said, "but I was always afraid of cold water. My birth father used to torture me with it when I was sleeping. This is the first time it's ever felt good."

For a few hours, anyway, removed from counseling and modern pharmaceuticals, the young man entered what Thich Nhat Hanh calls "the Pure Land," which he contends is always available to the mindful.

"The question remains, are we available to the Pure Land," the one that moves through us like a whisper, so fully, so completely, that we barely notice?

. . .

I PICK UP MY ROD AGAIN AND FLIP THE BAIL OPEN SO THE
line unspools, rapidly following the sinker to the depths. Turn
the handle and make the slack line taut. I would prefer to say
something to Senior that a fisherman would say, but instead let
fly: "Jesus's idea that the kingdom of heaven is within you: what
does this mean to you?"

He doesn't look up from the place where his line meets the
ocean. The expression on his face says, *What? You think you
can't pray and fish at the same time?*

"Look at your body," he says, "it's full of water. Jesus said, 'I
am the water of life. Greater is he who is in you, than he who is
in the world.'" Senior's line twitches slightly but his hand doesn't
flinch. He's not after something that's small enough to nibble.

"If you think about it," he says, "water proves everything."

I ask him what he means by this.

I wait for what seems like a long while, the wind filling
my eardrums with a womb-like white noise as the boat orbits
the blue hole. The engine idles. I stare at his eyes behind the
sunglasses and finally get him to look up from his line for an
instant, before he returns his attention to its rightful owner.

Alma's Diner

Magic is equated to the quality of attentiveness. Perhaps magic is . . . the ultimate attentiveness.

—JIM HARRISON

The lobster is good. It is lightly battered and fried and the firm white flesh veined with pink steams in my mouth as I chew. I look down at my plate at the remains of the crustacean and squeeze from a wedge of lemon a few drops of juice onto the tail. I have eaten the peas and brown rice, every grain; the conch salad and the slaw I have consumed, slathering up the remnant juices with fresh-baked bread: and I have saved the lobster, the entire thing, for last.

Everyone at the table—Linda, Delcina, Meko, William, Jeffrey—is eating lobster, except for the man who brought the lobsters up from the bottom and shone a lantern onto their slick backs. Hardened machinery of the dark. Senior nibbled on some conch fritters and fish fingers, but his meal is in a Styrofoam to-go box wrapped inside a plastic grocery bag. "I'm all full up," he says. I suspect he fasts at Alma's so that he can share with Nicey, who is watching the grandkids at home.

"And he was a pretty good fishing guide, too," Senior says, but his sons and grandson, fishing guides who moonlight as preachers, are talking boisterously about how long the Sunday service ran, and they don't hear him. If they're ignoring him it's only subtly, the way sons do a soft-spoken father, not trying too hard to listen over the single huge speaker that blares gospel R & B from behind the bar. He turns to me and shrugs. "He just told them, 'Throw it to the other side of the boat,' and they pulled up a net full of fish. A hundred fifty three!"

"Those guys must have been the worst kind of clients," I say of Jesus's disciples, relishing another bite of Alma's cooking. Its texture is perfect, clean; it snaps, moist in the mouth, and I'm reminded of how my grandmother used to say that we've all chewed on morsels of heaven but have either been too busied with dinner conversation or greedy for another bite to taste them fully. "I mean, the kind of client you have to tell everything to. They didn't think to try the other side of the boat? And fish counters, too!"

Senior brushes off my attempt at irreverence. "They were continually on the water. It was a way of life, the fisherman's life, so they had to know their way around a boat. Why they didn't think to try the other side, I don't know. Maybe they were just waiting for another miracle to occur near the water."

Jesus had already turned water into wine, Senior explains, and walked on water, and calmed the seas, and ordered Peter to buy from a man a fish that had a coin in its mouth, and was to sweat blood, among other water-related miracles. "Is it easier," I inquire, "to perceive miraculous things when you're around water?"

"I think it makes men more than they are in their everyday lives," he says.

"Say, Pa," Meko says. "Sorry to interrupt but when you caught those two permit on the same day with the Coca-Cola man, where was that?"

"It was way out near Red Shank, at this spot we used to call the Rocks."

"Yeah, we still call it that. I was out there today telling that story to my client and he didn't believe me."

"Wait," I say, grabbing Senior's arm. "You doubled on permit?"

"Yessir. Doubleheader. He and his partner."

A skilled angler who has traveled the world and caught several hundred bonefish may not be fortunate enough to ever land a permit, despite his best and most expensive efforts—the Yucatán, Belize, the Marquesas. Coveted and loathed because its capture requires not only skill but luck, the permit is the royal flush to the bonefish's straight. In precious metal terms: platinum to the bonefish's silver. For years management at Deep Water Cay Club had a standing bet with its guests: anyone who caught a permit on the fly got his week at the lodge for free, but the angler who agreed to the bet had to pay double if he didn't convert. Arguably the most desired fish on the flats, the permit is also the species most cursed by fishermen. An angler hooking and losing his first permit will be "ready for the rubber room," in the words of Thomas McGuane, who recounts his initial encounter with a pair of the mythical fish: "I wondered if I had actually seen them. I must have. The outline and movement remained in my head: the dark fins, the pale gold of the ventral surface, and the steep, oversized scimitar tails. I dreamed about them."

To speak it clearly: to catch one permit in a lifetime is a feat; to catch two permit in a lifetime is a matter of distinction; to catch two permit in a day on one boat is a matter of immense distinction; and to guide two anglers into a doubleheader on permit and land both fish is transcendent.

"A double," I ask again, piercing the penultimate bite of lobster with my fork. "On the fly?"

"My thoughts always get to drifting when I'm on the water," Senior says, an aside that seems to roll over everyone at the table like a quieting wave. "The wind whips over the boat and ruffles your jacket but it's kind of quiet. You can hear yourself think once you get past worrying whether the fish are gonna show. The Coca-Cola man wanted to try for permit—he was the vice president of the company, came every year when the moon was new in April—but he liked catching a little more than fishing, if you know what I mean. When

I'd poled for an hour past Burroughs, I staked us out 'cause I could see a ray in the distance. What I thought was a big bonefish rolled and flashed in the mud the ray stirred. Two, three hundred yards out.

"Maybe he had a rough night with the rum because when I told the gentleman to hop on deck, he got up like I told him to walk the plank. 'There's a ray coming right to left, about a hundred yards out,' I said. 'There's a bonefish behind that ray, but he'll eat your crab fly.'

"'I didn't tie a crab fly on,' he tells me. 'I left this Pink Puff on instead.'"

We guides at the table groan collectively—*Of course he did.* William motions for Alma to turn down the music.

"'And your leader?' I asked.

"'Ten-pound.'

"Way back at the docks, I had asked him to make sure he tied fifteen-pound to a crab fly for permit, but now we weren't equipped to handle anything bigger than a bone and there was no time to change. The ray closed in and was going to run straight across the bow at a good angle for a right-hander. I couldn't see well because the mud was three feet deep. 'When I slip the stake,' I said, 'I'm gonna swing the boat around so that you can cast right over the ray.'"

Parallel to the mud, Senior explains, so that the fly would stay in the feeding zone, his tableside offspring seconding his sound strategy with deep nods.

Senior continues: "'Land it just beyond the ray's tail and he won't spook.'

"A fish following a ray is like a man in the potluck line after church—he keeps eating. For a while it was ray, mud, ray, mud. No fish. I started to wonder if I'd been imagining things. Then a black tail broke the water. Permit."

Meko puts his fork down and leans back in his chair, then

takes the napkin from his shirt collar and wipes his mouth. He smiles like a child who has heard a grandfather's story before, as if his favorite part is yet to come.

"Now the Coca-Cola man had caught lots of bonefish," Senior says, "but he'd never caught a permit. If I said the word *permit*, he would have lost it—permit fever, when the guy gets shaky and forgets how to do the simplest things. So I said: 'That fish is about a rod length behind the ray. When you think you can cast past the ray, do it. Then let your fly sink two counts before you start to strip.'

"He got a pretty good sixty-foot false cast started but the fly landed smack on the big ray. I told him to pull it tight and hope it pops off clean. Thankfully he had tied a poor knot because it gave without much resistance and the leader popped straight-away and came back pigtailed.

"I didn't have time to get upset because suddenly I was seeing double: not one, but two permit tails shining above the mud, the second one about fifty feet behind the first. 'Get up on the bow right now,' I told the partner, 'and get some line off your reel.' At least someone had listened: he had tied on a crab fly made of carpet and rubber legs."

Offering cups of pudding from a tray, Alma hovers momentarily over my shoulder, but I'm too entranced for dessert. She sets the tray in front of Meko, whose eyebrows lift momentarily, and pulls up a chair. The night with its cool shawl shoulders in, the peepers growing louder.

"I had the Coca-Cola man's leader in my teeth and was knotting on some heavier leader while keeping the boat in line, pole pinched between my elbow and my side. I had a crab fly pinned to the brim of my hat. Who knows how long it had been there, if the hook point was rusted?

"'What are you doing?' he said.

"'Getting you ready, just in case.' Maybe he could see that

I had put my pipe in my pocket, which I rarely did, because he straightened up and for the first time all morning looked gamy.

"The ray was almost under us, so I told the partner to cast his fly over the ray. The wind coming over his left shoulder made the fly land perfect, a few feet in front of the permit. I was worrying about the ray's tail tangling the leader when I saw the permit tail up and told him to strip long.

"'Permit!' I said, and the men locked eyes with one another. Then I told the partner to climb down from the bow and the Coca-Cola man to get ready. He looked at me like I'd lost my mind. 'Another permit coming,' I told him. 'Eleven o'clock, forty feet. Cast high into the air so your fly won't spook.' While it was turned down tailing, he put it right on its nose. The line was tight before he stripped."

I picture the Coca-Cola man uniformed in the requisite khaki, sunburned, of course, and for amusement a tad portly, sweat beading at his temples, working with less time to think than act and laying out what might very well be the best cast of his life.

"The second permit ran north in the opposite direction of the first, so the lines stayed untangled. But when I started poling toward the first fish, the second fish would run against the pressure, and soon there wasn't much backing left on the Coca-Cola man's reel. So I poled toward that fish for a while and he gained line, but then his partner's spool would start to show, and I had to pole back to the south. Back and forth for at least twenty minutes. Tighten your drag down, I would tell one man. Now loosen yours, I would tell the other."

I can hear the reels' gears keening, one burst at a time, and the anglers' vigorous attempts to regain lost line. I imagine the two finned, pale-blue-gold shapes hovering opposite one another above swaying turtle grass. It's difficult to negotiate two worlds—one is hard enough—but like a man deftly balancing scales, Senior slides the skiff back and forth between the fish until his anglers gain leverage.

"The men were starting to get a bit delirious, famished for lunch. Sharks had come to the commotion, and I thumped one on the head with the end of the pole. By the time both permit were within twenty feet, I could count half a dozen lemons swooping around. We could have gone from two fish to no fish in seconds.

"The permit came to the bow on top of one another. I snatched the net out from under the bench and netted the first one—a twenty-five-pounder, two hands to hold the net handle, shoulders wide as a tire—and passed it to the Coca-Cola man, then tailed the second fish: a twin of the first."

I imagine Senior's arm hanging over the gunwale holding on to the tail above the fork, feel the anchor weight of that fish as it's lifted into a morphing shaft of light sent from the first star.

"The Coca-Cola man took a couple of pictures with me and those fish. He was going to put them in the mail. I never did see them. Maybe they're at the lodge somewhere. Afterwards he said if I hadn't worked the boat the way I did they would have never landed those fish. But who knows? I don't take credit for any of it."

The seafloor a dozen shades of yellow-blond, veined with swaying sargassum. With his right hand cupped under the brim of his hat, Senior stands and shades his eyes again, staring through the water's fractaled surface. What numinous countries below.

The Little Town

Observe that as he is one and simple, so he comes
into the one, which in the soul I have called
a little town.

—MEISTER ECKHART

There is a painting from the Campo Santo in Pisa that
I admire, an elaborate medieval fresco scene replete
with stags, falcons, angels, and priests. Near the center of the
mural—eight by six feet in real life but reduced to eight by six
inches on my computer screen—several maidens bathe in the
luxuriant courtyard of a castle, the home of three aristocrats
who have recently departed on horseback. In the upper right
corner, a barefoot hermit milks a goat near a small hovel that
sits apart from but not out of view of the castle. In various stages
of decay, the three skeletons lie slumped together in the lower
right corner, easy to miss.

The well-heeled hunters, one scholar's explication asserts,
have journeyed afield, are caught in a storm, and, while lost,
encounter their dead ancestors, who accost them for having not
been true to their past. The "three living/three dead" tradition is
a lasting one in medieval art, as is the appearance of the eremit-
ical figure who is frequently portrayed as living in a hermitage
not far from the castle. Often the hermit is a former chevalier
who has renounced that life, but still feeds advice to the young.
Aristocrats and courtesans wander to the hermit's house to ask
for his opinion on a text or important matter before returning
to the castle.

SENIOR WAS FAMOUS. NOW HE'S PENNILESS, LIVING IN A shack across the channel from the lodge he built. These days just a few working guides stop by, and the occasional traveling angler knocks to pay homage, but Senior isn't overwhelmed by callers.

When I think of him sitting down at the dock each evening, I recall a short parable Jesus offers in one of the Gospels, if a sentence can be called such: "A nobleman went into a far country to obtain for himself a kingdom and then returned." Dissecting this line, Eckhart says that meditation is our far country, and that we return from our solitudes with kingdoms, but allow these kingdoms to be usurped by our worldly desires.

On steeds named Delta, American, and Virgin, we angling noblemen journey to the East End of Grand Bahama and establish an immense sense of wonder at our surroundings; we hone our instincts, reconnect with vital wildness, engage with the simplicity of the senses, which Blake called "the chief inlets of the soul," reorder our priorities—but after a few days we return to our cubicles, to our old habits of excess, our daily, albeit unintentional, shunning of the natural world that, a short time ago, so thoroughly quickened us: wondering if our lives are what we have loved the most or what we have done the most.

Soon, in the mind's eye, Senior's little town at East End is just a falling sun pinholing into the horizon. There where he sits at the water's edge, with those wind-drawn diamonds at his feet.

I DON'T HAVE SENIOR'S PHONE NUMBER—I DON'T EVEN KNOW if he has a phone—but if I want to talk to him I just ring Delcina.

"Hello, 'Cina! It's Chris."

"Ah, Chris, how are you? Do you want to talk with Pa?"

"If it's not too much trouble."

"No, man, I can throw a rock at his house right now. Hold on just a minute."

And within the promised sixty seconds, Senior is on the line. "Yessir. How does it go it in the far north?"

He laughs when I say it was eighteen below zero recently in Montana, a cold far beyond his ken. He tells me about the time, when he was seventeen years old, that a few wispy clouds dropped snow on McLean's Town. The water grew so frigid that bonefish floated to the surface, bleary eyed, dead. This winter, though, has been all shirtsleeves, and the commercial snapper fishing's been quite good, he tells me. He's found a few monster lobsters near shore at night—"Big ones, man, ten-pounders."

I ask him what he was doing before I called. Oh, just greeting the morning, he says. Did it greet you back, I ask. I think it did, he says. I tell him of Meko's family's plans to visit Montana next summer on our generous shared client's dime, and Senior seems pleased. I ask about his grandchildren. Then he asks about my kids. I think of how when we first met, I had arrived in East End looking for an escape from my life, but found through a man and the place he tends deeper immersion, a way further in. Our true lives lie hidden from us; bonefish or not, perhaps we are always hunting ourselves. The hiss in the phone connection sounds like breaking waves, and the palpable impulse to express some gratitude slips through language's net. I picture Senior's gaze, its good weather. I tell him the children are well, quite feral and quite well.

WHEN I LAST SET BARE FEET ON THE FLAT JUST WEST OF Jacob Cay, I informed the man walking alongside me through the warm outgoing tide that I wanted some of my ashes scattered someday in our precise location.

"Let's find a GPS and mark the coordinates. I'm serious, Merv," I said, then instantly realized how hackneyed the remark must have sounded, that Mervin Thomas had doubtless heard similar sentiments from many anglers over the years.

"Yeah, man," he said, "that sounds good. But today you should fish. There's a pretty big school of bonefish down-light."

I scanned the underwater plain that seemed to stretch endlessly, mirage-like, before falling into deeper facets of green.

"How big of a school?"

"Oh. A thousand."

"A thousand! Where are they?"

"Where are they?" he said under his breath. "Where aren't they? They're covering the flat."

I stared harder but saw blond hummocks offset with shadow, the knobby expanse covered by water as clear as the air into which it evaporated. Some turtle grass undulating with the tide. Closer by, some random sponge and sea fan, a *Clypeaster* we call sand dollar, a miniature cactus field of hydrozoans. The near-waddling gait of a boxfish.

"Point them out to me," I begged.

Merv leaned over my right shoulder and grabbed hold of the rod in my hand. He swept it from left to right across the horizon entire. Right to left. Then left to right again. Everywhere.

Perhaps after a moment the tide dropped an inch, exposing them, or the sun fell a degree, south by southwest—whatever barely perceptible alteration in the seascape had occurred, it was said change, not some sudden advancement of my eyesight, that allowed the wide acre of bonefish tails, all bent and sun wicking, shining like uncut wheat lithe under the wind's labor.

We commenced with the harvest.

At times it was difficult to see the sand for the fish. After landing one I handed the rod to Mervin, who tried to decline my offer until I shoved my hands into my pants pockets. His open-elbowed presentation was gangly, surprisingly unrefined, but it was lethal: the fly would reach the end of its forward trajectory so high in the air, that falling imitation cast nary a ripple. His retrieval, just a twist of the left hand, the small curving motion you might use to peel an onion, teased the largest fish into playing. As he fought a five-pounder he'd hooked on his first cast, I asked when he'd last cast a fly rod.

"Five years ago," he said. "Or maybe ten."

That hooked fish sliced the flat-spanning school in half, and the sea of wheat split into two separate galaxies that orbited opposite one another until each galaxy's lead fish found the other and the whorls reconstellated.

Uncountable fish. Surfeit of stars seen on a clear night at sea. They lined up in the outgoing current, two deep, and simply opened their mouths to take shrimp and crabs tumbling off in the wash. By the time we had exhausted our territory, the tide was rushing off the shallows, a broad ankle-deep river falling steeply into an azure crevasse.

"I'll go and get the boat," Merv said, and we both glanced back at the small white craft on the horizon and laughed.

When he was out of earshot, I regarded the circumference of my surroundings and, in the cloistering noise of the wind and surf, let out a wild yelp of gratitude—to whom I wasn't exactly certain, but now I believe it was to the gentle hands of the water that had pulled a beleaguered man out of himself and set him back on earth.

I stood there waiting for a while.

I stood there half an hour.

I stood there forever, as the ocean forced me not to forget her. The water rushed off the edge of the flat as if off the edge of the world, taking me, or a part of me anyway, with it.

Sunrise. The man slings a casting net into the shallows. Landing, it makes the sound of a slight but intricate glass sculpture shattering.

Hand over wet hand, with the light warming his back, he retrieves the net, stretching the damp twine between a barnacled wooden post and a discarded capstan. Humming, he notes the net's deficiencies. There's one hole the size of his fist that a hawksbill likely tore with a flailing appendage, a few watch-dial-size openings cut by coral, and another vacancy as big as a boat's steering wheel. He could simply bring the mesh to the menders down on Sweetings Cay, but he's too thrifty to give them money for repairs he can make on his own: a reef knot here, a half hitch there.

He considers all the pilchards that have escaped through those holes, all the perch. Good for them, he thinks. Good for them.

Passing accompanists, seven terns shoot their high-pitched calls through the atomized salt and vanish into the horizon. Beyond the end of the dock across the sand from which the tide has just fallen, a wind picks up and etches something momentarily on the shallowest liquid page. In the beginning, a few moments ago, all the exposed—brain coral, finger coral, glistening bag of jellyfish on the growing spit of sand—was underwater. Now the big fish have slipped into the channel and only the most minuscule navigate the mounds of sand and rock.

He hums, pulls tight the first half hitch, and hums a little more a song heard only by small creatures, by water, wind, and light: this audience of his choosing.

Sources, Stimulants, Acknowledgments, and a Note on the Text

Body of Water is a work of creative nonfiction, a term of apparent ambiguity. To this author the term refers to a work that combines elements of memoir and reportage in search of story and truth. Narrative, fictional, and chronological liberties have been taken throughout its composition. Norman Maclean wrote, "As is known to any teller of stories . . . the act of writing changes them." Over the course of several years, I spoke with dozens of people over the phone and in person on the subjects of Deep Water Cay and David Pinder's life. Quoted material from these subjects, some of which appears anonymously, may be considered relatively verbatim though occasionally condensed for clarity. Any reader intimate with the East End of Grand Bahama will notice that names of locations have occasionally been altered; these shifts were made to protect the privacy of place and fishery.

My debts are great and my thanks are many both to works quoted within the text and to the following scholarly papers and books:

Albury, Paul. *The Story of the Bahamas*. New York: St. Martin's Press, 1976.

Allen, Thomas B. *The Shark Almanac*. Guilford, CT: Lyons Press, 1999.

Ault, Jerald, ed. *Biology and Management of the World Tarpon and Bonefish Fisheries*. Boca Raton, FL: CRC Press, 2007.

Craton, Michael. "Loyalists Mainly to Themselves: The 'Black Loyalist' Diaspora to the Bahamas, 1783–c.1820." In *Working Slavery, Pricing Freedom: Perspectives from the Caribbean, Africa and the African Diaspora*, edited by Verene A. Shepherd, 44–68. New York: Palgrave Macmillan, 2002.

Curren, H. Allen, and Brian White, eds. *Terrestrial and Shallow Marine Geology of the Bahamas and Bermuda*. Boulder, CO: Geological Society of America, 1995.

Curtis, Brian. *The Life Story of the Fish: His Morals and Manners*. Mineola, NY: Dover Publications, 1961.

Danylchuk, Andy, et al. "Aggregations and Offshore Movements as Indicators of Spawning Activity of Bonefish (*Albula vulpes*) in the Bahamas." *Marine Biology* 158, no. 9 (September 2011): 1981–1999. doi: 10.1007/s00227-011-1707-6.

Danylchuk, Andy, et al. "Ecology and Management of Bonefish (*Albula* spp.) in the Bahamian Archipelago." In *Biology and Management of the World Tarpon and Bonefish Industries*, edited by Jerald S. Ault, 79–92. Boca Raton, FL: CRC Press, 2007. doi: 10.1201/9781420004250.ch5.

Danylchuk, Andy, et al. "Effects of Recreational Angling on the Post-Release Behavior and Predation of Bonefish (*Albula vulpes*): The Role of Equilibrium Status at the Time of Release." *Journal of Experimental Marine Biology and Ecology* 346, no. 1–2 (August 2007): 127–133. doi: 10.1016/j.jembe.2007.03.008.

Eckhart, Meister. *The Essential Sermons, Commentaries, Treatises and Defense*. Translated by Edmund Colledge and Bernard McGinn. Mahwah, NJ: Paulist Press, 1981.

France, Robert Lawrence, ed. *Thoreau on Water: Reflecting Heaven.* Boston: Mariner, 2001.

Hannibal, Mary Ellen. *The Spine of the Continent: The Race to Save America's Last, Best Wilderness.* Guilford, CT: Lyons Press, 2012.

Johnson, Howard. *The Bahamas from Slavery to Servitude, 1783–1933.* Gainesville, FL: University Press of Florida, 1997.

Jones, Allen Morris. *A Quiet Place of Violence: Hunting and Ethics in the Missouri River Breaks.* Bozeman, MT: Bangtail Press, 2012. Jones's book is a treatise on the ethics of fair chase and blood sport, and stands as an excellent contemporary response to José Ortega y Gasset's seminal *Meditations on Hunting.*

King Jr., Martin Luther. "Drum Major Instinct Sermon." February 4, 1968. King Encyclopedia, Stanford University. http:// kingencyclopedia.stanford.edu/encyclopedia/documentsentry/ doc_the_drum_major_instinct/.

McGuane, Thomas. *Ninety-Two in the Shade.* New York: Vintage, 1995.

McGuane, Thomas. *An Outside Chance: Classic & New Essays on Sport.* New York: Houghton Mifflin, 1990.

Pape, Greg. *American Flamingo.* Carbondale: Southern Illinois University Press, 2005. Pape writes, of Audubon, "I knew he shot them to know them."

Rinella, Steven. *Meat Eater: Adventures from the Life of an American Hunter.* New York: Spiegel & Grau, 2012.

Russell, R. C. H., and D. H. Macmillan. *Waves and Tides*. London: Hutchinson, 1952.

Saunders, Gail. *Bahamian Society after Emancipation*. Kingston, Jamaica: Ian Randle Publishers, 2003.

Saunders, Gail. "Slavery and Cotton Culture in the Bahamas." In *Working Slavery, Pricing Freedom: Perspectives from the Caribbean, Africa and the African Diaspora*, edited by Verene A. Shepherd, 21–43. New York: Palgrave Macmillan, 2002.

Shepherd, Verene A., ed. *Working Slavery, Pricing Freedom: Perspectives from the Caribbean, Africa and the African Diaspora*. New York: Palgrave Macmillan, 2002.

Snyderman, Marty, and Clay Wiseman. *Guide to Marine Life: Caribbean, Bahamas, Florida*. Locust Valley, NY: Aqua Quest Publications, 1996.

Stokes, F. Joseph. *Handguide to the Coral Reef Fishes of the Caribbean*. New York: Lippincott & Crowell, 1980.

Todhunter, Andrew. "Bahamas Caves." *National Geographic* (August 2010). http://ngm.nationalgeographic.com/2010/08/bahamas-caves/todhunter-text. "Bahamas Caves" is the article referred to late in the book. Much of the technical information mentioned here is borrowed from Todhunter's thorough examination of blue holes.

Valdene, Guy de la. "Interview with Guy de la Valdene." By Marshall Cutchin. *MidCurrent*. Accessed March 29, 2016. http://midcurrent.com/people/midcurrent-interview-guy-de-la-valdene/. In addition to quotes obtained directly from

Valdene in phone conversations and e-mails, I quote liberally from Cutchin's fantastic interview in "The Old Feeling."

Zaleski, Jeff, ed. *Parabola* 34, no. 2 (Summer 2009). Much of the long litany on water's sanctity is culled from this issue, particularly "The Mirror of Heaven" by Geoffrey W. Dennis, and "There Is a River beneath the Skin" by C. Scott Ryan.

NUMEROUS CONVERSATIONS AND CORRESPONDENCES proved important in the completion of this book. My immense gratitude to: Chris Peterson of Hell's Bay Boatworks; author Mary Ellen Hannibal of San Francisco; medievalist Ashby Kinch of University of Montana, Missoula; Paul Adams of North Riding Point, Grand Bahama; Andy Danylchuk of the University of Massachusetts–Amherst; Reid Sanders of Memphis; J. B. Birdsall of Charlottesville; geologist Joseph Stasiuk of Grand Cayman; Gil Drake Jr. of Homosassa, Florida; Guy de la Valdene of Palm Beach, Florida; and various employees, current and former, at Deep Water Cay, East End, Grand Bahama.

Cristina Eisenberg of Oregon State University, formerly of High Lonesome Institute, provided illumination on the strange economic alchemy facing conservationists in this century and moment of mania.

Prescott Smith of Stafford Creek Lodge, Andros Island, is the son of perhaps the most recognized bonefish guide in the world, "Crazy" Charlie Smith. In 1968, with the help of investors, Charlie built and opened the Bang Bang bonefish club on Andros Island, the first Bahamian-owned fishing lodge, and is credited with having invented the most widely used bonefish fly in angling history: the Crazy Charlie, a simple, quick-sinking combination of calf's tail and flashy tinsel whose bead-chain eyes revolutionized the depth of water bonefish anglers could successfully ply. Known for his impromptu banjo playing and eccentric personality as well as his unparalleled knowledge of Andros Island bonefish habitat, the lovably immodest Smith has been the subject of numerous documentary films and magazine articles.

All members of the Pinder family—but especially Jeffrey, William, Delcina Pinder-McIntosh and Meko Glinton—displayed a gracious generosity with their knowledge. I can't imagine this book's having found its way into the world without their hospitality and kindness toward my research.

Thanks to friends and anglers Jefferson Miller, Peter Drake, Peggy and Chick Alexander, Brent Taylor, Daniel Gilliland, and Jeffrey Foucault, for sustained support and inspiration; to Larry Penrose for reminding me where home was; to Montanans Rich and Jill Brauss for an early roof and bed; and to the late Tom Harman for work, which so differs from a job.

Thanks to James Galvin for kindness and an "axe-handle" in *The Meadow*; Dan Gerber, Doug Stanton, and Jerry Dennis for sound counsel; Hannah Fries, formerly of *Orion*, who worked extensively on and published an essay titled "Chance Baptisms," portions of which appear in this book; to *Orion*'s Chip Blake for pointing me in the right direction; to editors James Babb of *Gray's Sporting Journal*, William Sisson of *Angler's Journal*, and Jim Stenson of the *Contemporary Sportsman* for publishing early versions of chapters. To Michiganders Joyce Bahle, the Popoffs, the Luyts, the Smiths, the Ungers, the Espinozas, the Chittles, Michael Delp, students and faculty at Interlochen Center for the Arts, and Jack and Julie Ridl—my gratitude for good harbor during the early work. Thanks to Debra Magpie Earling, Caleb Kaspar, Sam Michel, and Noy Holland, who provided quiet and essential work space. And to Susan O'Connor for vision and timely support. Huge thanks as well to the amazing stewards at Milkweed Editions.

Mary, Luca, Molly, Lily: even the saying of your names brings me comfort. Thank you for your patience and kindness toward this book. My mother and father, too, have supported this work in innumerable ways—my gratitude is deep.

Though he reportedly cannot cast a fly rod properly, editor Patrick Thomas is a sage guide—keen and kind—who knows precisely what to say when. He reined my long casts in when needed, and urged me to stretch the line when I threw too short. From dock to dock, his efforts have been essential and irreplaceable.

My immeasurable thanks to publisher and editor Daniel Slager, a poet turned nonfiction writer's dream, who reads with a translator's eye, which is to say, he despises approximation. Never has my work been met by such meticulous care, rigor, and graciousness in the same room.

Finally, this book could not been written without the guidance, generosity, and foresight of David Warnock, who, among other gifts, intuited a story in Senior's life and began to talk it out of me.

My deepest bows to David Pinder, the old man who is the sea, and to the ocean herself, vast water that righted this ship.

Erik Peterson

Born in Michigan, Chris Dombrowski earned his MFA from the
University of Montana. His publications include two collections
of poems, most recently *Earth Again*. His poetry and nonfiction
have been widely published in leading journals and magazines.
Also a fly-fishing guide, Dombrowski lives in Missoula, Montana.

milkweed
editions

Founded as a nonprofit organization in 1980, Milkweed
Editions is an independent publisher. Our mission is to
identify, nurture and publish transformative literature,
and build an engaged community around it.

We are aided in this mission by generous individuals who
make a gift to underwrite books on our list.
Special underwriting for *Body of Water*
was provided by Geoff and Janny Gothro.

milkweed.org